"A fascinating story and great lessons for every executive involved in managing cybersecurity."

—Phil Agcaoili, SVP Product & Security Innovation, Elavon, US Bank

"If experience is the best teacher, this is a PhD for any CEO or Corporate Director on cybersecurity risk. A great story easily understood by non-technical executives on one of the most significant breaches of our time."

—Bob Zukis, CEO of Digital Directors Network and USC Marshall School of Business Professor

The New Era of Cybersecurity Breaches

A Case Study
and Lessons Learned

GRAEME PAYNE

Copy Edited by Annie J from www.just-copyeditors.com

Cover Design by Melgraphics.

ISBN 978-1-950878-02-4 (Paperback)

Ordering information: Special discounts are available on quantity purchases by corporations, associations, and others. For details, contact the publisher at info@cybersecurity4executives.com.

Visit Cybersecurity4Executives at cybersecurity4executives.com

Published in the United States of America.

The New Era of Cybersecurity Breaches is dedicated to my two sons, Alexander and Miller, who inspire me, and encourage me every day. In tough times, there is no better support than from one's family.

Contents

Preface

I will never forget July 30th, 2017, a day after my 54th birthday. It was a Sunday and I had been out with my family enjoying a warm summer day in Atlanta, Georgia.

I tried to keep my business life and personal life separate and would only check my email during weekends once or twice. That Sunday—when I arrived home in the early afternoon—I picked up my phone and noticed several missed calls from our Chief Security Officer, Susan Mauldin. I immediately called her to find out what was up.

Susan advised me that overnight, her security team had identified a security incident where it appeared that an attacker had exfiltrated data from the ACIS Portal. I was the Chief Information Officer for Global Corporate Platforms at Equifax. The ACIS system was one of many that my team managed.

At 4 p.m. on September 7th, Equifax released a press release announcing a "cybersecurity incident" affecting approximately 143 million U.S. consumers. The press release was accompanied with a video from Mr. Richard Smith, Chairman and Chief Executive Officer of Equifax. In the video Mr. Smith said:

"This is clearly a disappointing event, and one that strikes at the heart of who we are and what we do. I deeply regret this incident and I apologize to every affected consumer and all of our partners. We all know the threats to data security are growing by the day and while we have made significant investments in cybersecurity, we have more to do and we will…Equifax will not be defined by this incident, but rather by how we respond...”

As expected, the story was soon picked up by the news media and the Equifax Data Breach became headline news for the next few days.

The atmosphere within the company when the breach was announced was one of shock and disbelief. No one wants to see the company they have worked for criticized and vilified in the news media and by politicians and pundits. I held several meetings with my team as did other leaders, asking our associates to stay focused on delivering customer service and supporting any requests we might get from legal or security teams as a priority.

There were the usual questions about whether the company would survive, would it be penalized, how did this happen, and so forth. Most of these, I couldn't answer. Then there were questions more personal in nature—was my own job secure, would we still be getting bonuses, and what would happen to my project? Some even asked, somewhat bizarrely, "how are you doing?"

The stock market reacted pretty quickly and Equifax shares traded down. The company had been enjoying a good run up in stock price over the last ten years and much of this was wiped out as the stock plummeted by 35%.

On September 26th, 2017, Mr. Richard Smith—the Chairman and CEO—announced his retirement.

Throughout the previous nine weeks, I had wondered how this incident might affect me professionally. I had seen my boss, the CSO and the

Preface

CEO all depart and I assumed those senior positions would most likely represent the "management accountability" for the incident.

Of course, this was not to be.

* * * *

This book is a case study of the 2017 Equifax Data Breach and other large data breaches that have occurred in the last several years. The book brings together what we know from the public record. The Equifax Data Breach exposed personal information of over 146 million Americans, remaining one of the largest data breaches of our time. The 2017 Equifax Data Breach is unique in that it has been the subject of several investigations by Congressional committees and regulatory agencies. The results of many of these investigations have been made public and provide us with a unique view of the facts and circumstances surrounding the event.

I wrote this book for two reasons.

Firstly, I wanted to bring together what we know from public documents and press coverage of the Equifax and other major breaches to provide a case study for executives and security professionals. By consolidating this information into a case study my hope is that you may be able to take away some tips to help in better managing your cybersecurity program.

Secondly, I wanted to share many of the key lessons that I learned, about how to manage cybersecurity and what to do when your organization has a cybersecurity breach. These lessons span the past thirty years of my consulting and professional life. Over that time I have worked with hundreds of companies, supporting them in their management of IT and cyber-risk.

This is not a technical cybersecurity book. There are plenty of great books that dive deep into the technical side of cybersecurity. This book is designed for executives, managers, security leaders, Boards of Directors and others charged with protecting an organization's important data and responding when things go wrong.

Implementing a sound cybersecurity program requires a combination of people, process and technical controls. Too much emphasis on any one of these, and the program may be at risk. In writing this book, I hope you will gain a better understanding of the challenges in managing cybersecurity, and use the lessons learned from the cybersecurity breaches to improve your own cybersecurity program.

The book is divided into three parts. Part I – *A New Era of Cybersecurity Breaches*, provides some context on the increasing occurrence of data breaches and the challenges of managing cybersecurity in the modern enterprise. Chapter 1, *The Rise of Cybersecurity Breaches*, provides context on how cybersecurity has evolved and why data breaches are becoming more common. Chapter 2, *The Challenge of Managing Cybersecurity*, discusses some of the common challenges in managing cybersecurity today and provides some foundational advice around building a cybersecurity program.

Part II – *The Equifax Case Study* consolidates what we know from the public record about the 2017 Equifax Data Breach. Using information drawn from public investigations, company filings, press coverage, and primary research, these chapters summarize the facts that are known and the views of others that have written on the topic. Chapter 3, *Who is*

Equifax, provides an overview of the credit reporting industry and how Equifax grew from a small Atlanta, Georgia-based company supporting shopkeepers, to a large data aggregator of digitized data about consumers in the U.S. and around the world.

Chapter 4, *Equifax Technology*, describes how technology innovation drove constant change at Equifax and explains the dispute and disclosure system that was attacked in the breach.

In Chapters 5, 6, and 7, I break down the specifics of what happened, how Equifax responded, the subsequent investigations, and the longer-term impact on the company.

Chapter 5, *The Cybersecurity Incident*, talks about how this cybersecurity incident was different and how the senior managers quickly engaged experts to help the company ready itself for the breach announcement. Chapter 6, *Going Public: Notification and Response*, discusses the Equifax public announcement on September 7th, 2017 and the post-notification response.

Chapter 7, *Challenging Times*, reviews the longer-term impacts of the breach on the company, including the financial costs, and how the company is transforming post-breach.

Part III – *Broader Lessons and Recommendations*, provides some additional recommendations on improving cybersecurity. In Chapter 8, *A New Path Forward*, I draw out some observations about what we should all learn from this and other major breaches that have occurred before and since the Equifax Data Breach. There are lessons learned for us as a society, for us as company executives, and for us as consumers.

Finally, in Chapter 9, *Improving Cybersecurity*, I share how I am now helping executives and Boards of Directors manage their cybersecurity risks through my company, Cybersecurity4Executives.

The book references many external sources and I have provided links to these for those of you that want to dig deeper into these sources. The links, while current at the time of writing, will ultimately become obsolete—as is the changing nature of the Internet—but I trust you can enjoy the book's content regardless.

Part I – A New Era of Cybersecurity Breaches

Chapter One –
The Rise of Cybersecurity Breaches

The Evolution of Cybersecurity

I was born at the end of the Baby Boomer generation and have been fortunate to live through such a tremendous time of technology innovation and transformation. When I entered the workforce in the mid-1980's, we were just starting to harness the value of computing technology within the enterprise.

I started my career as a financial auditor, working for Arthur Young (later Ernst & Young) in New Zealand. Many of my clients were running large IBM mainframe systems accessed via "green screen" terminals. Data was keyed in, processed by the computer programs and various printouts and reports provided the information needed to run the business.

The most challenging security issues then were around physical security to the data center and ensuring that the security management packages—restricting access to the systems and data (such as RACF, ACF2)—were correctly configured.

The other major concern was backup and disaster recovery.

What would happen if the mainframe crashed or the data center was destroyed? Most companies could not afford a full backup data center and many relied on third parties to provide "cold"[1] or "warm"[2] sites that they could use in the event of a disaster. No company had a Chief Information Security Officer, very few had CIOs. There were small IT functions that typically reported to the CFO or other administrative officer.

Bundesarchiv, B 145 Bild-F077889-0042
Foto: Reineke; Engelbert | 0. April 1988

The IBM Personal Computer debuted in 1981.

The IBM personal computer was released in 1981, followed a few years later by the Apple Macintosh. I recall we had one IBM PC in our office when I started. Within a few years, we would all have a PC or "luggable" computer on our desk.

---

[1] A "cold" site provides office space, but the customer provides and installs all the equipment needed to continue operations. A cold site is less expensive, but it takes longer to get an enterprise in full operation after the disaster.

[2] A "warm site" is a facility used to recover an organization's technology infrastructure when its primary data center goes down. Warm sites normally include equipment and infrastructure that can be easily configured to recover normal operations.

Chapter One: The Rise of Cybersecurity Breaches

Over the next decade, there was a tremendous growth in technology, including the advent of lower cost mini-computing systems from companies like DEC, HP, Sun and IBM. These systems allowed for smaller companies to start leveraging technology without the significant investment required for mainframe systems.

By the late 1980's and early 1990's, innovation was focused around the software that ran on these computers. Microsoft Windows created a new way for users to interact with systems using the graphical user interface. America Online in 1985 provided an early view into what would later become a highly interconnected world.

I started to see the possibilities of the interconnected world when I purchased my first modem. It allowed me to use the phone line to dial up and connect with various BBS (bulletin board services) and later, America Online. Early hackers started to use the same public phone system to "war dial" and find computer modems. Once a hacker (also known as "phracker") identified a modem they could try accessing the system or network, often using default passwords or brute force attacks.

Interestingly, as far back as 1967, as ARPANET – the predecessor to the Internet – was being rolled out, an engineer named Willis Ware wrote a paper called "Security and Privacy in Computer Systems". Ware headed the computer science department at the RAND Corporation, an Air Force-funded think tank in Santa Monica, California. Ware was concerned about the lack of security when multiple computers were networked together.

As the 1980's came to a close, we started to see commercial internet service providers offering an on-ramp to the new world wide web. As computers became more interconnected, new security risks arose.

Viruses and worms could now spread and propagate through the connected networks.

The Morris Virus (1988) was an early example that used the Internet to propagate itself and reach thousands of computers in a few hours, slowing down the Internet.

Security focus shifted to how to prevent viruses through anti-virus software. Companies also started to deploy simple packet-filtering firewalls to help block unwanted traffic from entering the network.

In the late 1990's, the widespread use of the Internet drove another phase of innovation. Companies could efficiently coordinate product design, manufacturing, distribution and sales all through computer systems and the networks that connected them. As the 1990's came to a close, there was a terrific amount of investment in the "dot com" boom. New business models were developed. Companies like Google, Facebook, and Amazon were starting around this time and would eventually become huge data brokers in their own right.

As the Internet became a place for commerce, security focus moved to the web applications. As businesses rushed to put functionality on the web, security teams were concerned about how these applications could be used to connect to the back-end systems. Attack and penetration services flourished as security teams sought some independent validation that these risks were real.

I had moved to Atlanta in 1996 and had started a security consulting practice within Ernst & Young. Many of our early projects were demonstrating just how weak most companies' Internet security controls were. A tremendous amount of capital started flowing into the information security space and a lot of great innovation occurred in the late 1990's and early 2000's.

In addition to a lot of protective solutions, I started to see emerging defensive technologies—intrusion detection systems, early monitoring solutions and the emergence of the managed security service provider.

Organizationally, leading companies started to establish more centralized approaches to information security. Some of my consulting work in the early 2000's was helping stand up a new information security function. In 1995, Citibank hired Steve Katz as its Chief Information Security Officer. Katz is regarded by many as the first CISO. It would be another ten to fifteen years before the CISO role became common in many organizations.

In 2002 Congress passed the Sarbanes-Oxley Act ("SOX") which had a significant impact on security. Suddenly financial officers and auditors were asking about segregation of duties within systems. Identity and access management became a hot topic for audit committees and financial controllers.

A few years later the first Payment Card Industry ("PCI-DSS") standards were issued and merchants were required to meet very specific security standards to be able to process credit card transactions.

By 2005 companies were well on their way to digitizing data and providing web-based services to their customers. In that year, 136 data breaches (55 million records) were reported by the Privacy Rights Clearinghouse[3]. Most records of data breaches start in 2005, although there were certainly data breaches before then.

---

[3] Privacy Rights Clearinghouse, https://www.privacyrights.org/

The New Era of Cybersecurity Breaches

The term "cybersecurity", while first used in 1989, did not gain significant traction until around 2013. Gartner even wrote a paper detailing how the term should be used. "Use of the term "cybersecurity" as a synonym for information security or IT security confuses customers and security practitioners, and obscures critical differences between these disciplines". According to the Gartner paper: "Cybersecurity encompasses a broad range of practices, tools, and concepts related closely to those of information and operational technology security. Cybersecurity is distinctive in its inclusion of the offensive use of information technology to attack adversaries"[4].

Over the last decade as companies have continued to march forward on digitization of everything, the cybersecurity risk profile has continued to change. Advances in mobility, social, cloud computing, micro-services, APIs, artificial intelligence and machine learning, just to mention a few, have significantly changed the risk profile. Cybersecurity professionals are faced with a much-expanded attack surface, a more sophisticated attacker, thousands of signals (alerts) from monitors, advanced persistent threats, malware, ransomware, credential stuffing and lots more.

According to MarketWatch the cybersecurity market is expected to reach $300 billion dollars by 2024, growing at 12% CAGR per year. Virtually every company has a security team and is investing in deploying security technologies to help prevent and detect unauthorized intrusions. In the last five years the financial losses due to cyber-attacks have risen by over 62%. There is also a worldwide shortage of cybersecurity talent.

---

[4] Joe Frascella, Cybersecurity vs Cyber Security: When, Why and How to Use the Term, http://www.infosecisland.com/blogview/23287-Cybersecurity-vs-Cyber-Security-When-Why-and-How-to-Use-the-Term.html

Data is Attractive to Hackers

One of the by-products of the digitization of everything is that companies have realized the immense value they can derive from data. Think about a company like Ford Motors. What is their business today? Sure, they design, manufacture and market various automobiles. Ford has also invested heavily in technology.

They have enabled their cars and trucks with onboard computing systems providing navigation, location-based services, and SOS help in case of emergency. They have Bluetooth, Wi-Fi and satellite connectivity. The car is now a computer on four wheels, constantly collecting, storing and sending data.

YouTube launched in 2005 and is now the second most visited website in the world. It has 1,300,000,000 users who upload 300 hours of video every minute. Its users watch 5 billion videos every day.[5] Just think about how much valuable data Google (owner of YouTube) is generating.

Companies that build large data repositories, whether it be structured data like Equifax, Experian, TransUnion, or Ford Motors, or unstructured data (YouTube, Google, Facebook) have a very valuable set of data. Not only is it valuable to the customers of these companies, but it is also valuable to bad actors (such as, hackers, criminals, and, nation-states).

---

[5] YouTube by the Numbers: Stats, Demographics & Fun Facts, 1/6/19, Omnicore, https://www.omnicoreagency.com/youtube-statistics/

The New Era of Cybersecurity Breaches

Since the beginning of the 21st Century there has been a tremendous growth in the use of technology in our business, government and personal lives. Companies have accumulated massive amounts of data about their customers, operations and markets. Businesses are highly dependent on their computer systems and networks. The Internet of Things is now connecting every conceivable device, generating even more data for collection, storage and analysis.

As all these changes have been happening, criminals, activists and nation-states have been improving their capabilities to utilize technology to attack companies and governments and to capture sensitive information they could use to further their objectives.

In the 21st Century, there have been numerous well publicized breaches (see chart). These involved major corporations being targeted for consumer information.

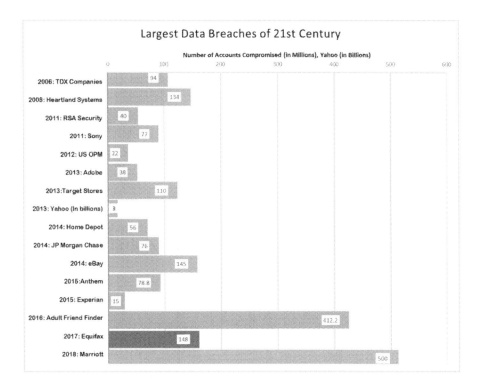

Yahoo experienced a series of breaches dating back to 2013, exposing more than 3 billion Yahoo user accounts. Names, addresses, dates of birth, passwords and security questions and answers were stolen. In 2013-2014, retailers Target and Home Depot both experienced breaches resulting in hundreds of millions of retail customer payment card details being stolen.

A data breach at JP Morgan Chase in 2014 compromised the data of 76 million households and 7 million small businesses. Information disclosed included name, address, phone number, and email addresses, and other information about users. In 2015, health insurer, Anthem— the second largest health insurer in the U.S.—suffered a data breach that exposed names, addresses, Social Security numbers, dates of birth and employment histories for nearly 80 million current and former plan members.

In September 2015, Equifax competitor, Experian, notified consumers of a breach in one of its servers that resulted in names, addresses, Social Security numbers, dates of birth, driver's license, military ID, and passport numbers of over 15 million consumers being exposed for a period of two years.

In September 2017, Equifax announced a cybersecurity incident that resulted in the exposure personal information of 143 million consumers.[6]

In November 2018, Marriott announced a massive data breach affecting 500 million guests. The hackers had access to the Starwood Hotels reservation networks for the previous four years. In addition to names, addresses, and credit card numbers, the hacker also gained access to passport numbers, travel locations and arrival/departure dates.

According to the Privacy Rights Clearinghouse there have been 8,983 publicly disclosed data breaches since 2005. The total records breached from these attacks are 11,583,824,031.[7]

In 2018, IBM and The Ponemon Institute released their 13th annual 2018 Cost of a Data Breach Study. The study reported that the global average cost of a data breach was $3.86 million. The average cost, globally, for each lost or stolen record containing sensitive and confidential information was $148 per record.

---

[6] The number was later updated to 146 million affected consumers.
[7] Correct as of time of writing. For up-to-date number see: https://www.privacyrights.org

The study also found that breaches are only getting bigger with the average size of breaches, based on companies surveyed, increased by 2.2 percent year after year.

There is no doubt that we are in a new era of data breaches.

Bad Actors

The data held by companies today is a prime target for many different "bad actors." Bad actors can be broken down into three broad groups:

1: Cyber Thieves

One group clearly comprised the cyber thieves who want your personal information so they can steal your identity and leverage that for financial gain. Today, much of this is driven by organized crime. They seek out valuable data by hacking into companies because it is too easy and too rewarding. The 2019 Global Risk Report issued by the World Economic Forum identified cyberattacks—the theft of data and money—as the fourth most serious risk behind natural disaster and war. Cybercrime is estimated to cost the global economy $6 trillion by 2021, and it has been reported that it is the fastest growing crime in the US.

Cyber thieves include mercenaries who constantly probe and attack companies to find weaknesses in their security controls and then exploit anything they find. Often, they gain access via vulnerabilities in web applications. Other times they use phishing attacks to try and gain credentials or to trick a user into visiting a website and without their knowledge downloading a piece of software that can further be used for reconnaissance, to gain additional access privileges or to hold the user's device, and maybe the entire company, ransom.

Cyber thieves will often be independent contractors. Once they gain valuable data such as credit or bank account numbers, they will offer these for sale on the Dark Web or receive a commission from the criminals who engaged them to do the hacking. The Dark Web is a part of the Internet which cannot be found through a search engine like Google, lying intentionally hidden to conceal and promote criminal activity. Some estimate the Dark Web to be 500 times larger than the surface web (the web that you and I can search through Google).

2: Trophy Hunters

Trophy Hunters target high profile individuals to gain information about them and then use that to embarrass or harass them. They may use the information to extort a ransom. Companies like Equifax obviously have data on high profile politicians, service men and women, as well as government employees in sensitive roles, such as intelligence officers, national security personnel, and uncover agents).

If a hacker can gain sufficient personal information about these individuals, they may be able to track their movements, open and close accounts in their name, gather sensitive information about them that could be used to blackmail them, or impersonate them. One example happened in March 2013 when Equifax, TransUnion and Experian acknowledged intrusions into their systems after information about celebrities and high-profile figures ended up on the Exposed website.[8] Credit reports and sensitive data on Paris Hilton, First Lady Michelle Obama, former Secretary of State Hillary Clinton and FBI director Robert Mueller were obtained using fraudulent and unauthorized

---

[8] Robert Westervelt, 3/13/13, Equifax, Other Credit Bureaus Acknowledge Data Breach, CRN, https://www.crn.com/news/security/240150683/equifax-other-credit-bureaus-acknowledge-data-breach.htm

access. The hackers were able to utilize publicly available data on these individuals to answer security authentication questions.

3: Espionage

The third group that was of particular concern were nation states. Over the last few years, there has been a big increase in nation state cyberattacks. Nation state attacks are designed to gain information to help in espionage and cyber warfare. They are often playing a "long game" and may use the information they have gained over many years or even decades. Nation states are particularly concerning because of their ability to mass resources against a single target or group of targets. Take for example the NotPetya and WannaCry malware attacks that occurred in 2017, creating significant disruption to corporations and government agencies around the world.

According to the Verizon Data Breach Investigation Report which reviewed data from 86 countries and over 41,000 incidents, 23% of bad actors are identified as nation-state or state affiliated. Organized crime account for 39% of attacks.

Chapter Two –
The Challenge of Managing Cybersecurity

Identifying, mitigating and managing cybersecurity risks in today's environment is a challenging task. Despite companies spending millions of dollars protecting their data, intellectual property and systems, we face well-resourced and determined adversaries. What can we learn from the major data breaches of the last fifteen years?

First, every company is a potential target for attack. A quick review of the list of companies that have been breached shows every industry is susceptible – financial services, healthcare, manufacturing, education, government, retail, telecommunications, utilities, and more. Also, size is not a factor, with reports of over two-thirds of small and medium-sized businesses experiencing at least one security incident over the past two years.

While many data breaches relate to consumer information, there are increasing examples of cyber attacks that have geopolitical motives or intent.

Managers often fail to understand their company's sensitive data flows, where sensitive data resides, and who has access to it.

Second, a company's risk profile is constantly changing. Senior leaders need to understand the risks faced by the company and constantly manage how these risks are being mitigated or addressed.

The New Era of Cybersecurity Breaches

The challenge is to continually measure and monitor cyber-risk across the entire company. Cyber risk is dynamic – threats and vulnerabilities are constantly changing and require constant monitoring and risk mitigation adjustments. Understanding the threat landscape and being able to identify potential attacks on a continuous basis is required.

Implementing a sound cybersecurity program with multiple lines of defense is important. Investing in monitoring and detection capabilities is a critical component of the cybersecurity strategy.

Senior management and the Board should actively engage in the cybersecurity discussion. In many cases, those responsible for communicating about cybersecurity, have difficulty in communicating the risks and challenges in business terms.

Third, while there are great technical solutions to help companies manage and mitigate risk, in the end most data breaches result from human failure. For example, the most common causes of data breaches are:
1. Weak or stolen credentials
2. Phishing
3. Application or system vulnerability
4. Physical loss/theft
5. Human error (such as sending email to wrong person)

Building the right level of cybersecurity awareness among the company employees remains a key challenge.

Fourth, complexity in the information technology environment is a challenge. Many companies have a mix of older ("legacy") technology and newer state-of-art technology. Systems are highly interconnected with data flowing across networks and systems. Many companies are executing "digital transformation initiatives" that include increased automation, connectivity and integration across supply chains, manufacturing, distribution and customer journeys. Many companies are migrating to cloud-based services.

At the same time, security technologies are evolving. Integrating these technologies into the fabric of the IT environment is a major challenge. Some companies, especially small and medium-sized businesses, have not made the required investments in security technologies and continue to rely on manual or informal processes for cybersecurity.

Finally, inevitably controls will fail and your company will be breached. With sound detection processes you should be able to identify and react quickly, closing the hole before too much damage occurs. However, sometimes detection may fail or be delayed and you have a major breach. Companies that have well-structured incident and crisis management response processes and protocols and have exercised and tested them, will be in better position to contain and recover from a significant security incident.

What can companies do to help mitigate the risks associated with increasing data breaches?

Senior Management and Board Focus on Cybersecurity

The last several decades have seen several periods of sustained growth and tremendous amounts of technology innovation. As more processes have been digitalized companies have accumulated significant amounts of data.

The New Era of Cybersecurity Breaches

As all these changes have been happening, criminals, activists and nation-states have been improving their capabilities to utilize technology to attack companies and governments and to capture sensitive information they could use to further their objectives.

As these changes were occurring, have senior leadership teams and Board of Directors pivoted their focus enough toward protecting and securing the data? Are they asking the right questions? Do they have the expertise to really evaluate the responses they were receiving? Does cybersecurity receive the same focus as growth initiatives, new acquisitions and company performance?

The bottom line is that cybersecurity is a business risk not an information technology risk. Senior Management and the Board need to manage cybersecurity risk just like they do other business risks.

One of the first steps is ensuring they have the right expertise in their company to advise them on their cybersecurity risk. Today, this is typically the Chief Information Security Officer ("CISO"). Among the responsibilities of the CISO should be:

1. Articulating cybersecurity risks to senior management and the Board, including keeping abreast of developing security threats, and helping the board understand potential security problems that might arise from acquisitions or other big business moves.
2. Developing and implementing a cybersecurity strategy, including securing funding to execute the plan. This includes planning, buying, and rolling out security hardware and software, and making sure IT and network infrastructure is designed with best security practices in mind.

3. Establishing and maintaining security policies and standards that define expectations, roles, responsibilities and procedures for the implementation of sound cybersecurity controls.
4. With other managers, building a cybersecurity culture. This should enable all employees and managers to understand the critical roles they play in helping to keep the company secure, identify suspicious activities, and assist in incident response.
5. Establishing and managing a security operations capability that includes real-time analysis of immediate threats, and triage when something goes wrong.
6. Ensuring that only authorized people have access to restricted data and systems.
7. Implementing programs or projects that mitigate risks such as vulnerability management and patch management.
8. Establishing cybersecurity incident response processes, conducting regular exercises, and executing procedures in the event of a security incident.

In Chapter 9, I cover more details about the important role the Senior Management and Board play in cybersecurity.

Establish and Maintain Good Security Policies

All IT security control frameworks (e.g., ISO 27001, NIST CSF, CobIT, CIS Controls) refer to the importance of security policies within the organization. Security Policies provide the requirements or expectations for securing certain aspects of the enterprise. Organizations develop a set of policies that align with their overall governance models and culture. By writing these down and communicating them, it is clear what is required and by whom. Typically, security policies will be built around a policy hierarchy. The names and definitions may vary but generally have between three and five levels where the top-level policies are general statements of principle and the lowest level are procedural steps or guidelines specific to a set of technologies and serving as an instructional guidance to system administrators.

Example Policy Hierarchy

Policies - Broad statements of principle, change infrequently, approved at senior level, apply organization-wide

Standards - Focus on requirement and controls, describe how to implement policy, detailed process requiring conformity

Procedures – State how to comply with a standard, step-by-step process, uses instructions, references automated processes/tools

Guidelines - Best practices, encouraged but not required, helpful hints, user guides

---

I have seen over the years several different approaches to the development of security policies. In some organizations, all the policies are contained in one comprehensive document. The document includes both policy statements—broad statements of principle—as well as very specific security standards and procedures. The challenge with this approach is that it can be difficult to consume or use. Finding the relevant policy requires digging through a lot of detail.

Another common approach is to create separate policies to cover specific policy areas, for example, an organization might have separate policies on end-user computing, physical security, corporate security, and so on. In this way, documents would be easy to identify and understand; roles and responsibilities would be more clearly defined;

and, policies—and how to implement them—would be in separate standards and procedures documents.

Some companies have their Board of Directors or a senior management policy committee review and approve the policy documents. This adds the "tone from the top" perspective and can help with implementation.

Let's use the example of a patch management policy. Ever since computer systems were first developed, there has been a need to install fixes or patches to address functional or security gaps identified in software. We all see this happening to our own devices where we are constantly getting system updates. Patch management is like fixing the leak in the roof or replacing the rotten timber before it gets worse and the leak turns into a major project.

Items that might be included in a patch management policy would be:

1. Defining a patch management *Policy Manager*. The Policy Manager's primary responsibilities might include; develop and maintain the policy and supporting standards that operationalized the policy; implement controls and checks to measure the effectiveness of the policy; and, approve exceptions to the policy.
2. Define a *Patch Management Process Owner*. The patch management process owner responsibilities might include:
   a. Establish a patching process that defined dependencies and approvals to ensure successful and regular patching;
   b. Establish procedures that IT and Business teams must follow in order to achieve regular and effective patching;
   c. Manage an escalation process when needed;

    d. Work with Legal and Compliance staff to demonstrate compliance with regulatory requirements, contractual commitments, industry standards, and on implementing Corrective Action Plans as required;

    e. Work with HR and additional stakeholders as appropriate to incorporate and coordinate the training program and content to cover Patching responsibilities;

    f. Report the status of patches during quarterly business reviews and for Risk Committee review.

3. Provisions related to special situations and how to obtain exceptions to the policy requirements. For example, there may be legacy assets that cannot be patched for operational reasons and additional security controls may be needed.

4. Specify when the policy should be reviewed and updated and who is responsible for review and update.

5. Define key roles and responsibilities with operational responsibility for patching systems. For example:

    a. **Business Owner** - the business person who used the system. This person will be informed of when a patch event is scheduled and will approve any production system downtime required to install a patch.

    b. **Application Owner** - the IT person who was responsible for ensuring an application or system is patched.

    c. **System Owner** - the IT person responsible for actually installing the patch. This person would have access to the system to be able to test and install the patch.

    d. **Scheduler** - an IT person who coordinated the change process and scheduled the patch installation.

    e. **Security Team** – would notify appropriate parties of a need to patch systems and verify that patch had been installed.

6. Define communication requirements or protocols for ensuring patching information flows to the appropriate parties.
7. Define patching requirements. For example, critical patches may need to be installed on external-facing systems within 48 hours, while low risk patches might be required as part of routine system maintenance.

Documenting and publishing a Patch Management Policy is an absolute key step in improving an organization's patch management process. The policy should clearly define the patching expectations and the roles and responsibilities of key participants in the patching process.

However, for the policy to work, it requires further steps to be completed:

1. A robust implementation plan to bring everything into compliance with the requirements of the policy
2. Published standards, procedures and guidelines to help execute the process and educate parties on their roles and responsibilities
3. An ongoing monitoring process to ensure compliance, detect and remediate instances of non-compliance, and update the policies, standards, procedures and processes as required.

When a required security patch is not applied the system may be vulnerable to attack. It takes time and resources to test, deploy and document patches. Some patches require systems to be taken offline or restarted, causing interruptions in service which must be planned and scheduled. According to a study by Kenna Security, the median time to remediation is 100 days.[9] That is a long time to be exposed.

Many security companies report that 70-99% of exploits are based on known vulnerabilities, many of which have patches available to fix the vulnerability. Some report that these vulnerabilities have existed for three of more years.

Organizations need to ensure that there are robust processes supporting security policy requirements. Key stakeholders need to understand their responsibilities and to be trained. Automated tools can help ensure consistent process execution and should be used rather than relying on human intervention with a higher probability of execution failure. Processes should be closed loop with metrics and measures providing feedback on process execution effectiveness. There should be clear escalation paths when patches are not installed on schedule.

Management should also receive regular metrics and updates to monitor progress.

Build and Maintain Comprehensive Asset Inventory

An IT asset inventory is an outcome of a sound IT Asset Management program. The International Association of Information Technology Asset Managers (IAITAM) defines IT Asset Management as "...*a set of*

---

[9] Kenna Security, 3/12/19, Prioritization to Prediction: Volume 3: Winning the Remediation Race (https://resources.kennasecurity.com/research-reports-3/prioritization-to-prediction-winning-the-remediation-race-2)

business practices that incorporates IT assets across the business units within the organization. It joins the financial, inventory, contractual and risk management responsibilities to manage the overall life cycle of these assets including tactical and strategic decision-making.[10]

IT Asset Management requires the implementation of processes and technology to record and track hardware and software throughout its lifecycle from procurement through to disposal/retirement.

Most organizations today use asset management discovery tools that provide detailed data about hardware and software assets, including operating system versions and patch levels, installed on various servers and computing devices. These can be complemented with security scanning and monitoring tools to identify devices connected to the network and potential vulnerabilities on these devices.

The IT asset inventory can also be enhanced with information about the business context of the IT asset. For example, the business process that the IT asset supports (such as finance, operations, sales), the physical location of the asset, and whether the asset is Internet-facing. This information can help security and IT professionals make informed risk decisions about patching criticality and prioritization.

For an IT asset inventory to be comprehensive, it needs to be able to identify all components of the system, including middleware. Today, there are automated software composition analysis tools that can interrogate systems to determine the specific open source and third-party components used in the system. Keeping the IT asset inventory up-to-date requires strong integration with other supporting processes

---

[10] International Association of Information Technology Asset Managers (IAITAM) website. https://iaitam.org/what-is-it-asset-management/

such as procurement, change management, and configuration management.

Once a vulnerability is announced and/or a patch is available, IT operations and security personnel need to quickly identify the impacted systems and ensure they are patched. Establishing and maintaining an accurate inventory is a challenging task but is vitally critical to the security of any organization.

Implement Prevent and Detect Controls

The most effective security model is one where there are multiple layers of protection and detection – often referred to as "defense in depth" or "layered security". There are many security frameworks that can help you identify the specific controls that you should consider implementing in your environment. See Chapter 9 for further discussion.

Some of the common controls (not a complete list) are listed in the table below (in alphabetical order, not implying any priority or importance).

Protect Controls	Detect Controls
Asset Inventory	End Point Detection & Response
Data Encryption	Incident Response
File Integrity Monitoring	Intrusion Detection
Identity and Access Management	Logging
Malware Protection	Penetration Testing
Multi-factor Authentication	Security Monitoring/SOC
Network Firewalls	
Network Segmentation	
Patching	
Secure Configuration/Hardening	
Security Awareness Training	
Security Testing of Software	
Vulnerability Management	

When implementing prevent and detect controls you need to consider three important factors: (1) process; (2) technology; and, (3) people. To illustrate this let's take an example of implementing a centralized digital certificate system.

Digital certificates are extensively used in many companies to support encrypted file and data transfer. Web servers use a security protocol known as SSL (Secure Socket Layer) to encrypt traffic between the web server and browser.

SSL requires a digital certificate to be installed on the web server. A digital certificate is a piece of code that has been signed by a certificate authority who has validated the identity of the certificate holder. Digital certificates are issued for a limited time (normally no longer than twelve months) after which they expire.

In a large company, it becomes challenging to manage potentially thousands of digital certificates that all have different expiry dates. To help solve this, companies implement a centralized certificate server which tracks all certificates in the company and ensures they are renewed and updated when required.

To effectively implement this control requires the deployment of the centralized digital certificate management system (technology), registration of all the current digital certificates into the management system (process and technology), education of administrators and security personnel (people), metrics and dashboards to monitor non-compliance (process), and procedures for revocation and reissuing of certificates (process and technology).

In our highly connected world, it is also important to have visibility into what is happening on your company network, devices and systems. The importance of having a strong security monitoring capability cannot be overemphasized. Networks and systems are continuously generating "events" or signals that should be sent to a central monitoring system.
A good example here is identifying and remediating vulnerabilities in your network. Every company should have processes and technology in place to identify and remediate security vulnerabilities.

On a daily basis, your company's cybersecurity team will receive many updates and information notices about vulnerabilities. For example, in 2017, over 16,000 new vulnerabilities were reported by US-CERT.[11] Your security team will need to wade through the multitude of notices

---

[11] US-CERT is the U.S. Computer Emergency Readiness Team responsible for analyzing and reducing cyber threats and vulnerabilities, disseminating cyber threat warning information, and coordinating incident response activities. It is part of the Department of Homeland Security.

and determine which vulnerabilities and patches should be prioritized. This requires that you know what systems and sub-systems that are running in your network. This data is normally found in an asset and software inventory.

You then need closed-loop processes to notify all the system administrators that manage the impacted systems. Your policies and standards should set expectations for when certain patches and fixes to systems be made to remediate a known security vulnerability. Here is an example:

Patch Category	Patch Deployment Timeline
Critical	Installed within 48 hours from the time of release or time frame agreed with security
High Risk	Installed within 30 days from the time of release or time frame agreed with security
Medium Risk	Installed within 90 days from the time of release or time frame agreed with security
Low Risk	Installed within normal patching rotation, but within at least 1 year from the time of release or time frame agreed with security

It is important that high-risk systems (such as those exposed to the Internet) are patched in a timely manner. Your processes should provide for the vulnerabilities to be tracked, prioritized, and monitored to ensure timely remediation.

Exceptions to patching or vulnerability remediation should be identified, and approved at a senior management level. Metrics and measures should be provided showing the state of vulnerability exposure – identified, closed, open, and exception-approved.

New systems, and changes to existing systems, should be required to be scanned for security risks prior to deployment.

At any time, your company is likely to have a certain number of un-remediated vulnerabilities. Management should be made aware of the extent of un-remediated vulnerabilities, the amount of time the systems have been un-remediated, and the risks associated with un-remediated vulnerabilities.

In some cases, this may be outsourced or co-sourced to a third-party secure operations center (SOC). This is an area where artificial intelligence and machine learning will likely play an important role in the future. Having the right tools, processes and people to monitor activity is important, but also is the standardized processes for how to deal with incidents. For example, removing from the network or quarantining an infected device.

Robust Response Processes

Every organization should have a well-documented and practiced cybersecurity incident or data breach plan and process. The probability that your company will be breached is close to 100%. The time to prepare for this is not when a breach occurs but well before.

I discuss this topic more fully in Chapter 9.

Closely Monitor Legacy Systems

I use the term "legacy system" to describe outdated computer systems, programming languages or application software being used instead of available upgraded versions or technologies. A legacy system is not necessarily defined by age. Legacy may refer to lack of vendor support or a system's incapacity to meet the organization's needs.

In theory, it would be great to be able to have immediate access to the most advanced technology available, but every company has some form of legacy system in their environment. Business managers make risk-based decisions every time they choose whether to replace/upgrade a legacy system or to new build new capabilities.

Legacy systems become an operational challenge when they can no longer be maintained, supported or improved. When this happens, they will also likely become a security risk.

Legacy systems can be expensive to maintain. Often, they also have legacy software running on old and antiquated hardware, the systems may not be well-documented or understood, and the longer they remain, the harder it is to maintain, improve, and expand their capabilities because of the general lack of understanding of the system. The staff who were "experts" on the system may have retired or forgotten what they knew about it. Most likely, there will be a lack of—or maybe missing—documentation about the system, further exacerbating the challenge of fully understanding it.

Legacy systems may have vulnerabilities in older operating systems or applications due to the lack of security patches available or applied. Commercial software vendors like Oracle and Microsoft only provide support for their products for a limited time. After that time, security and operational patches are either very expensive or most likely, unavailable. Integration with newer systems may also be difficult because new software may use completely different technologies than the legacy systems, while programmers may have to write special integration routines, further adding to the legacy burden.

So here is the rub: you have three forces competing for the next technology investment dollar and you have three choices. Where you invest that next dollar (or more likely many dollars) requires a tradeoff. You need to balance the benefits and the costs. This is exactly what senior leaders do all the time.

Replace Legacy Systems		Invest in New Capability		Address a Risk Issue
Pros: + Reduces legacy operating costs. + Reduces legacy risk.	**O R**	Pros: + Faster to market. + Drives revenue.	**O R**	Pros: + Reduces risk exposure. + Potentially reduces future cost.
Cons: - May require customer coordination. - No revenue impact. - Additional transition costs.		Cons: - Doesn't reduce risk or legacy operating costs.		Cons: - Forgoes revenue, increases costs.

Part II – The Equifax Case Study

Chapter Three –
Who Is Equifax?

"If you think of the largest library in the world—the Library of Congress—well, Equifax handles 1,200 times that amount of data every day." Mr. Richard Smith, Chairman and CEO, Equifax[12]

At the time of the 2017 Data Breach, Equifax held data on almost 1 billion consumers and nearly 100 million small and medium-sized businesses. It had nearly 100 million active employee records in its databases. The company had records covering 20 trillion dollars of property data and 20 trillion dollars of wealth data (annuities, mutual funds and equities).

A 100-Year-Old Company

When I started working at Equifax, I was surprised to find out that the credit reporting industry was over 200 years old.

Back in the early-1800's, shopkeepers in England formed "mutual protection societies" and began swapping information on customers who failed to pay their debts. Shopkeepers believed that by exchanging information about customers who did not pay their debts, they would know who the unscrupulous customers were and not extend them any further credit.

---

[12] Mr. Richard Smith, Chairman and CEO, Equifax speech to Terry College of Business at the University of Georgia (https://www.youtube.com/watch?v=lZzqUnQg-Us)

Mutual protection societies started forming throughout the United Kingdom through the rest of the 19th century. The concept of mutual protection societies did not gain traction in the United States until around the mid-1850's. In the US, early credit reporting societies took a different approach. They saw the benefit of collecting bad debt information and selling it for a profit, rather than just sharing data among shopkeepers for their mutual benefit.

The history of Equifax starts with two brothers, Cator and Guy Woolford from Woolford, Maryland. "They started their credit investigations by going door-to-door among merchants, asking about their customers and noting the findings in ledgers. Cator, a former bank employee, and Guy, a lawyer, employed simple notations to reflect merchants' comments about their shoppers' payment habits: "Prompt," "Slow," or "Requires Cash."[13]

In 1898, the Woolfords moved to Atlanta, Georgia hoping to make credit reporting their new career. They formed the Retail Credit Company and began compiling credit information into a book, *"The Merchant's Guide"*, selling copies to merchants for $25 (about $755 in 2019 currency). Retail Credit Company posted a loss of more than $2,000 in its first year of operation but sold many more books the following year.

In other cities, organizations similar to Retail Credit Company formed to collect and sell information about consumers, to protect business owners from racking up irrecoverable debt. By 1900, there were some

---

[13] Krista Reese, Equifax, 4/20/2019, New Georgia Encyclopedia, https://www.georgiaencyclopedia.org/articles/business-economy/equifax

fifty credit reporting companies in the U.S., centered around the major cities.

In 1901, the Retail Credit Company expanded into the moral hazard market[14], selling credit information to life insurance companies. By 1913, the company was incorporated and began reporting for automotive liability insurance.

By the 1920's, more than 20% of purchases made in U.S. department stores were made on credit. Motor vehicles were becoming more popular and due to their high cost were frequently purchased on credit. The Retail Credit Company continued to grow through the depression years and by 1930, had 81 branch offices throughout North America.

In the early days of the Retail Credit Company, information was collected using "investigators and inspectors" who would interview merchants, neighbors and acquaintances to gather data about such things as a consumer's health, moral beliefs, acquaintances, vehicle use, church attendance, race and sexual habits, and home environment.

---

[14] Moral hazard is the risk that a party has not entered into a contract in good faith or has provided misleading information about its assets, liabilities, or credit capacity. In addition, moral hazard also may mean a party has an incentive to take unusual risks in a desperate attempt to earn a profit before the contract settles. In the context of life insurance, moral hazard means the likelihood that an insured consumer's behavior will change as a result of purchasing a life insurance policy and that change will increase the chance of a loss. Life insurance companies look to ensure that the act of purchasing life insurance does not make it more likely for someone to end their own life or the life of another.

There were many claims that "this information originated from potentially unreliable neighbors and acquaintances."[15]

Paraphrase of an early credit report:
"Peter Mullen has done business in the same store for the last 35 years and made some money; owns a lot in Chicago, heavily mortgaged; is the oldest of two children; has lately married his second wife; is professionally a Methodist; and enjoys a general reputation for honesty." [16]

Following World War II, the U.S. Government lifted many of the wartime limits on spending, and the modern consumer economy began. Gross national product, a measure of all goods and services produced in the United States, jumped from about $200 thousand million in 1940 to $300 thousand million in 1950, and to more than $500 thousand million by 1960. More and more Americans now considered themselves part of the middle class.

The number of automobiles produced annually quadrupled between 1946 and 1955. A housing boom, stimulated in part by easily affordable mortgages for returning servicemen, fueled the expansion. Credit became the lifeblood of the U.S. economy. Not only would consumers use credit for large purchases like automobiles and homes, they would also use credit to purchase televisions, washers and air conditioners to place into them. Retail Credit experienced rapid growth during the

---

[15]   Rachel   Bunker,   9/18/17,   The   Equifax   Way, https://www.jacobinmag.com/2017/09/equifax-retail-credit-company-discrimination-loans
[16] The Breach Podcast, S2 Ep 1, published by Carbonite, https://www.carbonite.com/podcasts/breach/s02e01-Equifax-data-breach

period of post-war prosperity, and by the mid-1960's, had 300 branch offices and 1,400 sub offices.

Credit records were now kept manually; imagine rows and rows of file drawers containing thousands of index cards. Each office and sub-office had individual cards for each consumer in their specific city, town, or locale. When a merchant would need to determine whether a consumer had a "credit issue", the merchant would call the local Retail Credit Company branch and speak to an agent. The agent would take down the particulars of the consumer and then a runner would go to the file drawers, access the relevant index cards, and return these to the agent.

The agent would then read the credit record of the consumer over the phone to the merchant. This must have been an amazing operation to watch, reminding me of the way we used to locate books in the school library. Every book had a physical location referenced using the Dewey Decimal System. Files of index cards were used to look up a book title or author, and direct you to the physical location of the book on the library shelves. Keeping the index cards updated was a major task of the librarian.

Around the time I was born in 1963, computer systems were starting to be used by corporations to automate transactions-intensive operations. Retail Credit Company saw the benefit of automating the data held on index cards to help manage and search the vast amount of data it had collated over many decades. Retail Credit Company became an early adopter of this new technology. Computerization of credit records would reshape the credit reporting industry over the next fifty years.

At the same time that Retail Credit Company was computerizing its records, there was "significant controversy surrounding the CRAs because their reports were sometimes used to deny services and opportunities, and individuals had no right to see what was in their file."[17]

There were reports that investigators, incentivized by Retail Credit Company to fill quotas of negative information on consumers, fabricated negative information or included incomplete information in updates to credit files.

During the 1960's, there were increasing calls by academics, news media, and consumer advocates to regulate the credit reporting industry. Congress was also concerned about the role of the credit reporting agencies, especially as data previously held in local offices and sub-offices was now being combined into nationwide databases, and hearings were being held to both better understand the issues and to discuss how to protect consumers.

Retail Credit Company was an early adopter of the new mainframe systems starting to be used in Corporate America. The company began migrating data from written index cards to electronic data records in the mid-1960's.

Retail Credit Company's extensive information holdings, and its willingness to sell them to anyone, attracted criticism of the company in the 1960s and 1970s. Columbia University Professor Alan Westin wrote an article critical of Retail Credit Company in *The New York Times,* after reviewing a sample of credit files. He concluded that the reports included "facts, statistics, inaccuracies and rumors" about every phase

---

[17] The Fair Credit Reporting Act (FCRA) and the Privacy of Your Credit Report website, Electronic Privacy Information Center. https://epic.org/privacy/fcra/

of an individual's life, including "marital troubles, jobs, school history, childhood, sex life and political activities."

This article and Professor Westin's testimony helped drive Congress to pass the Fair Credit Reporting Act 1970 with the goal of promoting "accuracy, fairness and privacy of consumer information contained in files of consumer reporting agencies."

As a result of the Fair Credit Reporting Act in 1971, Retail Credit and other credit reporting agencies came under the regulatory jurisdiction of the Federal Trade Commission ("FTC"). It was not long before the FTC accused the company of rating its employees based on how much negative information they could find about consumers. Retail Credit Company pledged to monitor its procedures more carefully, and the government halted its investigation.

Retail Credit faced another investigation in 1973, when the FTC accused the company of monopolistic practices. Again, charges were dropped; by that time (1982), national computer databases made information that was once available only regionally, accessible nationwide. The company's name changed to Equifax[18] in 1979, and many believe the name change was to counter the memory of the continued government investigations.

---

[18] It has been reported that the name originated from "equitable factual information" (see: https://www.creditrepair.com/blog/credit-score/credit-bureau-history/)

A Typical 1960's Retail Credit Company Office[19]

As computing technology continued to evolve through the 1970s-1980's, Equifax was able to accumulate more and more electronic data on consumers and businesses. During this time, they acquired many of the previous local credit reporting agencies that operated on a city or county basis. At the same time, two other credit reporting agencies were rapidly expanding in the US: TRW (which would later become Experian) and TransUnion. By 1986, Equifax had data on 150 million consumers in twenty-eight states.

---

[19] (Slade, Harvey E. (Harvey Eugene), 1909-1975. Office of Retail Credit Company. 1966. Black & white photoprint. State Archives of Florida, Florida Memory. Accessed 20 Apr. 2019. <https://www.floridamemory.com/items/show/47836>.)

Chapter Three: Who Is Equifax?

By the late 1990's, industry consolidation resulted in three major nationwide credit reporting agencies—Equifax, TransUnion, and Experian—controlling the market. Today, in addition to the "Big 3," there are hundreds of specialty credit reporting agencies also collecting consumer information and providing credit (consumer) reports.

Computing technology facilitated another development in the credit reporting industry, the "credit score." Credit scores had been around since the 1950's but really came into prominence after two statisticians—Bill Fair and Earl Isaac—made a number of correlations between those behaviors making a person a good credit risk and those making them a bad credit risk. Ultimately, this led to the FICO score which was introduced in 1989 and is still a key evaluation tool in lending decisions[20].

---

[20] The major CRAs including Equifax have also developed their own scores but FICO remains the industry leading score.

A large data center circa 1965. The Retail Credit Company data center would have looked similar with large tape drives containing programs and data. (Source: NASA)

In the 1990's, Equifax started to expand internationally with acquisitions in the United Kingdom, France, Canada and Chile, among others.

In 1997, Equifax spun off its insurance data exchange—a business in which it had been active since 1901—to create ChoicePoint.

ChoicePoint obtained and sold to more than 50,000 businesses the personal information of consumers, including their names, Social

Security numbers, birth dates, employment information, and credit histories.

Interestingly, ChoicePoint would come to suffer its own data breach challenges a few years later. In 2005, a breakdown in ChoicePoint's internal controls over third parties led to the unauthorized disclosure of 163,000 consumers' confidential information to identity thieves. At least 800 cases of identity theft were reported as a result of the ChoicePoint data breach. While this seems minimal in today's environment, it was considered a big deal in 2005:

"At first, the ChoicePoint security breach seemed not only ordinary but almost insignificant.... But somewhere along the way, the ChoicePoint saga became the spark that caused an explosion.

Maybe it was the fact that this wasn't a hack. Personal information of nearly 145,000 people wasn't stolen from ChoicePoint. In fact, the company sold the information to inadequately vetted bogus businesses—this when the company itself helps other businesses verify creds. Maybe it was that the people whose information was compromised weren't customers of ChoicePoint, just accidental citizens of the vast databases of the Alpharetta, Ga.-based information broker.

Maybe it was the way that ChoicePoint behaved after the breach: from an initial, bumbling response that smacked of marketing, to a changing story about what had happened and how the company was responding, to the revelation that top executives had sold millions of dollars' worth of stock between the time the fraud was discovered and when it was announced to the public.

The New Era of Cybersecurity Breaches

Or maybe it was this last twisted bit of irony: ChoicePoint Chairman and CEO Derek V. Smith had recently written two books about how individuals can protect themselves in the information age.

You can't make this stuff up."[21]

The Federal Trade Commission investigated the ChoicePoint data breach. ChoicePoint signed a consent decree with the FTC, agreeing to pay $10 million in civil penalties and $5 million in consumer redress to settle the FTC's charges that its security and record-handling procedures violated consumers' privacy rights and federal laws. The settlement required ChoicePoint to implement new procedures to "ensure that it provides consumer reports only to legitimate businesses for lawful purposes, to establish and maintain a comprehensive information security program, and to obtain audits by an independent third-party security professional every other year until 2026."

"The message to ChoicePoint and others should be clear: Consumers' private data must be protected from thieves," said Deborah Platt Majoras, Chairman of the FTC at the time. "Data security is critical to consumers, and protecting it is a priority for the FTC, as it should be to every business in America."[22]

I find the numerous parallels between the 2005 ChoicePoint breach and the 2017 Equifax Data Breach fascinating. There were widespread calls

---

[21] Sarah D. Scalet, The Five Most Shocking Things About the ChoicePoint Data Security Breach, 5/1/05, CSO Magazine, (https://www.csoonline.com/article/2118134/compliance/the-five-most--shocking-things-about-the-choicepoint-data-security-breach.html)

[22] FTC Press Release: https://www.ftc.gov/news-events/press-releases/2006/01/choicepoint-settles-data-security-breach-charges-pay-10-million

for universal federal privacy legislation following the ChoicePoint breach in 2005. To date, no such federal legislation exists for U.S. corporations.

Through the early-2000's, the Equifax business remained largely focused on credit reporting—providing credit reports and scores to lenders, lessors, employers and insurers.

An Aggressive Growth Strategy

In December 2005, Richard ("Rick") Smith, a former executive at General Electric ("GE"), became Equifax's Chief Executive Officer. Rick had been mentored by Jack Welch, who had served as Chairman and CEO of General Electric between 1981 and 2001 and had led GE's value to increase 4,000%.

Rick Smith brought a lot of the "GE thinking"[23] over to Equifax. What he found was a company that was 97% in credit reporting, mostly in U.S.[24], generating moderate returns but susceptible to fluctuations in the mortgage and credit-granting industries, with growth rates at 1%-2% per

---

[23] In his book on leadership, Jack Welch identified eight principles of leadership. Many can be seen at work in the way Richard Smith led Equifax as CEO. (See: https://www.inc.com/dana-severson/these-8-simple-rules-of-leadership-from-jack-welch-are-more-important-now-than-ever-before.html)

[24] Equifax 10-K report stated that 82% of the revenue and 89% of the profit was attributable to the U.S.

year. The market value of Equifax when Smith started as CEO was approximately $3B.[25]

Smith's initial assessment of the company was that the company was a "slow growth company" with a "culture of entitlement", highly regulated, and largely in a "duopoly [sic]" with limited innovation.[26]

Rick Smith started on an aggressive growth strategy and believed the way to differentiate in the market was through unique data assets. If Equifax could secure these assets, they would be able to drive more revenue and topline growth. It would also help change the culture. His mantra was: "Gather as much data as possible and find new ways to sell it."[27]

Smith's first acquisition was a big bet. He invested $1.2B to acquire TALX Corporation in 2007. TALX based in St. Louis, Missouri, was a leading provider of human resource and payroll-related services and specialized in automated employment and income verification as well as unemployment tax management. At the time TALX had over 9,000 clients, including three-fourths of Fortune 500 companies. These clients provided salary details of their employees and gained access to the income verification and employment records of nearly half of all American workers.

---

[25] Immediately prior to the 2017 Equifax Data Breach, the market value was approximately $18B.

[26] Richard Smith speech to University of Georgia Terry College of Business

[27] Stacy Cowley & Tara Siegel Bernard, As Equifax Amassed Ever More Data, Safety Was A Sales Pitch, 09/23/17, The New York Times
https://www.nytimes.com/2017/09/23/business/equifax-data-breach.html

In 2009, Equifax paid $124 million for IXI Corporation, a company specializing in collecting, analyzing, and delivering consumer wealth and asset data, further expanding Equifax's unique data assets.

Smith started to implement plans to change the Equifax culture. He introduced new sales discipline, built a leadership program, and established a product innovation program known as NPI (New Product Innovation). The NPI team was charged with finding new ways to leverage the increasing data assets that Equifax was acquiring. NPI built between fifty and seventy-five new products every year. The team was tasked with generating 2-3 percentage points of organic revenue growth per year.

Under Smith's leadership, the company made a total of seventeen other acquisitions throughout the world. The significant growth in revenue and profitability under Smith's leadership provided the capital to aggressively acquire new businesses. Each year, the company aimed to add 1-2 percentage points of growth from acquisitions. One key such U.S. acquisition was the purchase of Computer Science Corporation (CSC) credit reporting agency business for $1 billion in 2012. CSC held credit files in fifteen states, covering 20% of the country's population.

In 2014, Equifax acquired Veda Corporation—a leading provider of credit reporting services in Australia and New Zealand—for $1.7 billion. The plan was that this would serve as a launching point for expansion into other countries in Southeast Asia. Equifax's strategy was to acquire companies where Equifax could be either the number one or number two player in that country.

Equifax 10-Year Performance ($m)

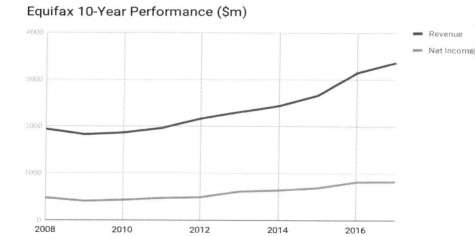

When I joined Equifax in April 2011, the company was just beginning to enjoy the benefits of these investments. By 2017, Equifax was generating $3.4 billion in revenue and growing at 8-10% per annum, compared to the 1-2% prior to Smith becoming CEO. Equifax had a market capitalization of approximately $18B immediately prior to the 2017 Data Breach. The significant growth and market leadership were not going unnoticed. Market analysts were very positive about the future prospects of the company.

Expanding Data Assets

A consumer credit system allows consumers to borrow money or incur debt, and to defer repayment of that money over time. Access to credit enables consumers to buy goods or assets without having to pay for them using cash at the time of purchase.

Chapter Three: Who Is Equifax?

Nearly all Americans rely on credit to make everyday purchases using credit cards, obtain student loans, gain approval for telecommunication or cable services, and make major life purchases such as cars and homes.

In order for this system to be efficient and effective, there must be a mechanism for a merchant to evaluate a consumer's creditworthiness. In earlier times, a retailer could often rely on the reputation of the consumer. But as cities and towns expanded and we became more mobile, there needed to be a more reliable method. This is where U.S. credit reporting associations began in the late 1800's.

Today, this is a highly sophisticated eco-system. Individual consumers do not voluntarily provide data to Equifax, rather data furnishers who are banks, auto lenders, utilities, telecommunications companies, and employers provide data about their consumers and employees to Equifax (and the other CRAs).

This data includes the consumer's name, date of birth, address, Social Security Number, loan amounts, payment history, outstanding balances and payroll data. Equifax performs some front-end data quality checks on the data and then use the data to update consumer records in various data exchanges.

The records can include the consumer's credit report, their employment record, and records related to telecommunications or utilities accounts. Equifax also records information about delinquencies, bankruptcies and claims. Up until the breach many Americans had not heard about Equifax and certainly about the information it had on them.

Typical Data Furnishers
Banks
Credit Unions
Insurance Companies
Utilities
Telecommunications
Cable Companies
Auto Lenders
Employers
State Governments

This valuable consumer and employee data is used by Equifax to produce models, scores, insights, reports and other digital products and services. Many of these products and services are sold to the same data furnishers that provided the information to Equifax for free.

Businesses use consumer data provided by Equifax to identify and manage financial and transactional risks. Lenders rely on credit reports when making loan decisions. Insurance companies use credit information to set insurance premiums. Employers use credit information to screen potential employees. Utility and telecommunications providers use credit data to determine deposit requirements for new customers.

Examples of data received by Equifax from data furnishers

Name and address

Date of birth

Social Security Number

New accounts opened

Balances on open accounts

Closed accounts

Employer

Salary/wage data

Employment start and end date

Mortgage lender, principal amount, outstanding balance

Many federal agencies use identity verification services provided by Equifax. The Healthcare Marketplace uses Equifax data to help validate income eligibility. The Inland Revenue Service uses Equifax data to help provide identity verification and validation. Many companies also use Equifax data for fraud detection.

Businesses also use credit scores to help make lending decisions or pre-screen consumers for offers. A credit score is a numeric value designed to predict a variety of financial behaviors. The concept was first developed by FICO and today, the two major providers of credit scores are FICO and VantageScore.[28]

These credit scores are generated using data in the Equifax (and other CRA) credit report databases. Equifax (and other CRAs) also have their

---

[28] The VantageScore model is managed and maintained by an independent company, VantageScore Solutions, LLC, formed in 2006 and jointly owned by the three bureaus (Equifax, Experian and TransUnion)

own proprietary credit scores similar to FICO. Credit scores are frequently used to pre-qualify or screen consumers for services. Each company uses a proprietary algorithm to calculate their credit score and so your score is likely to vary based on the algorithm and data used by each CRA in its score calculations.

Since the CRAs became regulated by the Consumer Finance Protection Bureau ("CFPB") in 2012, the CFPB regulators have taken an intense interest in the calculation of these scores because of the key role they play in determining whether consumers can gain access to credit. Many commentators have been critical of the use of credit scores, claiming inherent bias and discrimination against certain sectors of the population. New companies have started, developing new scores not based on the traditional models.

Equifax also provides marketing segmentation data to business customers. For example, you may frequently get letters from an airline offering you to enroll in a credit card program. Most likely you were identified as a pre-screen, eligible target consumer using data from Equifax.

Types of Products and Services

Credit reporting

Fraud monitoring

Employment verification

Analytical insights

Marketing targeting & segmentation

Merged (Tri-Merge) credit reports

Alerts

Decisioning tools and services

Identity verification

The rapid growth in the digitization of everything we do has significantly benefited Equifax. The company has become a giant data exchange. On one side are data furnishers who for the most part, freely provide information to Equifax and other credit reporting agencies, and these furnishers range from banks—like Bank of America, or Wells Fargo—to telecommunications companies like AT&T and Verizon.

Each day, Equifax receives terabytes of data which it runs through various data cleansing tools and processes before updating consumer and business records in its multiple data exchanges. Data is keyed and linked to tie data from different sources together for a particular consumer or business. In this way, Equifax has built what they described as the "360-degree view of a consumer" as shown on the next page.

The Equifax 360-Degree View of a Consumer[29]
(**Bolded** data = data assets unique to Equifax)

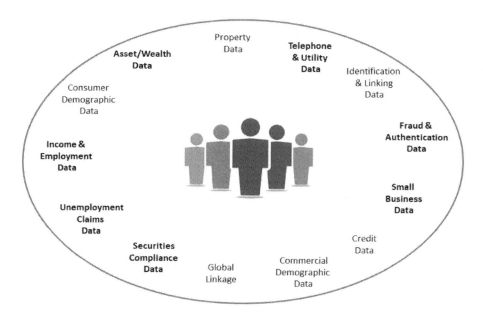

With this wealth of data resources, Equifax has been able to build various products and services by repackaging the data, adding insights, and selling the products to many of the same businesses that provided the data for free.

The growth in Equifax data assets can be seen in the following table. Consumer data increased by over 400% between 1986 and 2017, and the breadth of data collected increased significantly.

---

[29] Data sources disclosed in Equifax investor presentations

Equifax Growth in Data[30]

Records:	1986	2005	2012	2017
Consumers	150m	400m	600m	820m
Businesses			80m	91m
Employee	*Not a focus of company*	*Not a focus of company*	200m	278m
Trade Accounts			4.5B	5.75B
Public Records	*No data available*	*No data available*	100m	201m

So, Equifax and other credit reporting agencies have been able to accumulate massive amounts of data on consumers and businesses. Because of the virtually zero cost of input data, Equifax only needs to cover the costs of housing the data, developing new products, and product delivery (which today is virtually all electronic). Everything else is operating profit. Equifax operating profits (before interest and tax) are from 40-60%+ depending on the product.

To date, credit reporting agencies have focused on *structured data* - information with a high degree of organization, typically information included in a database and readily searchable. The next challenge or opportunity that credit reporting agencies are working on is how to

---

[30] Data sourced from Equifax investor presentations and 10-K reports filed with the Securities & Exchange Commission

leverage the massive amounts of *unstructured data* that exist on individuals and businesses.

<u>Examples of Unstructured Data</u>
Web browsing history
Social media posts
Youtube videos
Location tracking data

The explosion in connected devices including the interconnected "Internet of Things" (IoT) such as home devices, monitors, industrial control devices, wearables and so on will generate a significant amount of new data sources. Research firm IDC estimates there will be 163 zettabytes[31] of data stored by 2025. This is a ten-fold increase from an estimated 16.1 zettabytes in 2016.[32]

Connected device technologies will be able to tie an individual to a device and then generate relevant data about the individual's usage, movement, health and more. How will credit reporting agencies like Equifax be able to use this tracking and usage data?

The large credit reporting agencies are also investing significantly in building giant data lakes. These data lakes bring together data from all the various sources discussed above and provide an analytical sandbox for customers to conduct analysis and predictive modeling.

---

[31] One zettabyte is 1 trillion gigabytes

[32] David Reinsel, John Gantz,and John Rydning, November 2018, Data Age 2025: The Digitization of the World From Edge to Core, IDC Corporation Study sponsored by Seagate, https://www.seagate.com/files/www-content/our-story/trends/files/idc-seagate-dataage-whitepaper.pdf

Equifax invested significant money in Cambrian (Data Insights), their analytic database, employing hundreds of data scientists to identify ways to monetize the data and develop models and predictive analysis. Think of this like a crystal ball where you can peek into and try to see the future...maybe identify early risk of increased credit defaults or an impending economic downturn. As Artificial Intelligence and machine learning matures, the value of this data and what it can tell companies will be an incredible and valuable resource.

* * * *

So, like many companies, Equifax had assembled massive amounts of data, particularly in the last twenty years. In 2003 the company first mentioned in its annual 10-K filing with the Securities and Exchange Commission, that the security of its data and technology posed a business risk.

Chapter Four –
Equifax Technology

The Evolution of Technology

When Equifax started digitizing the consumer credit file in the mid-1960's, the company built its main credit reporting engine, ACRO. The system was designed and built to leverage the power of the new IBM Mainframes being delivered at the time.

As computing technology evolved in the latter part of the 20th and early 21st Century, Equifax built and delivered its products on newer technology platforms.

The company had been growing through many acquisitions, both within the U.S., and internationally. Paralleling the build-up in the data that credit reporting agencies and other data brokers was accumulating was an increasing concern by governments and regulators regarding consumer privacy. From the 1980's on, governments were placing increasing regulations on the processing and movement of personal information. For Equifax, this meant that in most countries, it needed to run separate data centers and systems for that country. Personal data needed to reside in-country for the most part. So, each time Equifax entered a new country, a new data center was added to the growing list of systems and data centers that needed to be operated and managed.

Equifax launched its web-based business customer portal (ePORT) in 2002 to deliver its services to customers. As the Internet became accepted as a vehicle for product delivery, Equifax moved more of its products to the web. In 1999, Equifax launched its direct-to-consumer business targeting consumers with credit monitoring and identity protection products.

In 2004, Robert ("Rob") Webb joined the company as Chief Information Officer. Rob set about to transform the IT systems. He drove a significant amount of IT outsourcing, moving the operations and support of many critical systems to offshore providers in India. This was a popular strategy at the time as the cost of maintaining and developing technology (especially mainframe systems) was increasing and managers were seeking ways to reduce operational costs.

Rob Webb also established a centralized information security team bringing together security functions that had previously been scattered through the various Equifax business units. Rob saved the company millions of dollars through cost-cutting, consolidation of systems, and strategic outsourcing. At the same time, a significant number of new products and product enhancements were released.

In September 2005, Tony Spinelli joined Equifax as the first Chief Information Security Officer. I had worked with Tony when we were both at Ernst & Young. He was very involved with the eSecurityOnline product that we had developed to help companies track assets and vulnerabilities. The tool would later evolve into ArcherGRC and become a leading IT GRC (Governance, Risk & Compliance) platform. Tony had been a CISO at First Data prior to coming to Equifax.

Tony Spinelli developed a strategy for creating a true global security function, centralizing many of the departmental efforts and implementing a plan to build an ISO 27001-compliant security operation. ISO 27001 was one of the leading information security frameworks at that time, and an international standard issued by the International Standards Organization. It was largely based on the British Standard BS7799.

The standard described an "information security management system" that organizations should have in place. It also contained a laundry list of "best practice" controls that should be implemented for effective information security management. Spinelli presented the Equifax Board of Directors with a three-year, $15M plan to reorganize IT security across the enterprise. Tony also hired some great resources and built out what many regarded as a leading information security function.

Later Tony Spinelli would spearhead the move of the Global Security team to report to the Chief Legal Officer, Kent Mast.

The topic of where cybersecurity should report in an organization is one that is frequently debated in the security and the IT community. According to a 2017 report from the Ponemon Institute, 50% of Chief Security Officers report to the CIO, while only 8% of CSOs report to the general counsel. Other surveys indicate a trend for more CSOs to report directly to the CEO.[33]

---

[33] PWC, Strengthening Digital Society Against Cybershocks: Key Findings from the Global State of Information Security Survey, 2018, https://www.pwc.com/us/en/services/consulting/cybersecurity/library/information-security-survey/strengthening-digital-society-against-cyber-shocks.html [hereafter referred to as "PWC Study"]

Kent Mast retired from Equifax in 2012 and was replaced by John "J" Kelley. Kelley had been a long-time partner in a local legal firm. Tony Spinelli left Equifax in early-2013 and a search began to find a replacement. After several months, Susan Mauldin was hired as the new CISO. Susan had previously been at SunTrust Bank and First Data where she also had been the CISO. Susan continued to report to J Kelley.

Dave Webb – who succeeded Rob Webb in 2010 as Chief Information Officer – recognized the significant amount of legacy technology and the need to start transforming to common infrastructure and platforms. Over the next few years, Dave led the push to standard platforms— building a set of reusable technology platforms that could be deployed to each country or business. This concept of "write once and deploy many times" followed the same transformation many companies were going through at the time.

At the same time, the IT network and infrastructure needed to be changed. New technologies (virtualization, storage networks, grid computing) and the resulting reductions in the cost of compute and storage would allow Equifax to better manage the sprawling data and systems in a more cost-effective manner.

The Dispute & Disclosure System: ACIS

In 1970, the U.S. Congress passed the Fair Credit Reporting Act ("FCRA"). The FCRA is designed to protect the integrity and privacy of a person's credit information. It requires credit reporting agencies, and the entities that report credit information to those agencies, to make sure all information is fair, accurate and confidential. Prior to this, consumers had no real right or ability to remedy errors appearing on their credit files.

The FCRA also provides for consumers to be able to file a dispute with a credit reporting agency if they believed their credit file contains an error. The credit reporting agency is required to notify the data furnisher of the dispute. The data furnisher has twenty-one days to investigate and report back to the credit reporting agency before the credit reporting agency is required to communicate the outcome of the investigation to the consumer.

When the FCRA was passed, Equifax had to build systems to manage this dispute process. Equifax built a system known as ACIS (Automated Credit Investigation System). ACIS initially was designed to be used by call center agents to log details of the dispute and then forward the details to the data furnisher. When ACIS was first designed, it was primarily focused on addressing the requirements of the FCRA.

Slowly, state governments and regulators started developing their own rules regarding how credit reporting agencies should handle disputes and provide free credit report disclosures in their specific state. For example, special provisions were created for active service personnel or parents in child custody arrangements. Some states allowed credit reporting agencies to charge for credit report disclosure, some mandated the amount to be charged, and others required free credit report disclosures in certain situations.

Later, as the Internet evolved, the ACIS application was extended to provide an online web portal for consumers to file disputes electronically, report identity theft, request a security freeze or request a copy of their credit report.[34] The online portal was effectively a web server displaying forms and information with which a consumer interacted, and it fed this information into a back-end database. The web server included a piece of software known as Apache Struts. Apache Struts is an open-source web application framework for developing Java web applications and is widely used by large corporations.

By 2017, the majority of requests were being made via the ACIS Dispute and Disclosure Internet portal at equifax.com. The consumer would access the portal, enter identifying information, complete questions designed to validate their identity, and then enter the details of the dispute or reason for the disclosure.

Once the dispute was logged, the system would create a notification to the data furnisher and send this using an industry-managed system known as e-OSCAR.

e-OSCAR (Online Solution for Complete and Accurate Reporting) was developed by Equifax, Experian, TransUnion and Innovis.

ACIS was also used as the system to request a security freeze (also often referred to as a "credit freeze") and to report identity theft. Depending on the state in which a consumer resided, certain rules and fees applied to utilizing these features. A security freeze locked your credit report and did not allow others (generally) to access your credit file and perform a "hard inquiry"—such as when you are requesting credit. A

---

[34] Changes to the FCRA in 2003 required the nationwide credit reporting agencies to provide one free credit report to a consumer each year. These are accessed via annualcreditreport.com. In addition, certain states require a copy of a credit report be provided to the consumer in certain situations. These specific state-mandated situations were managed through the ACIS Dispute and Disclosure portal.

security freeze did not lock your file from pre-screening searches and certain other regulated inquiries.

To support a request for disclosure, dispute, or to log an identity theft, the consumer was often required to provide supporting information such as their driver's license, letters to data furnishers, evidence of paid or settled bills, or police reports. The online web portal provided the capability for consumers to upload images or files of these items.

Following the Dodd-Frank Act 2010, the Consumer Finance Protection Bureau ("CFPB") gained regulatory oversight of Equifax. The CFPB took a particular interest in the dispute and disclosure process. In 2012, the CFPB launched an online consumer complaints portal. Prior to the breach in 2017, the CFPB had received over 60,000 complaints about Equifax, with the majority of consumers complaining about incorrect data on their credit file.

The ACIS web portal, part of the legacy ACIS system originally developed in the 1970's, was the system attacked by hackers in March 2017. Equifax later revealed that the root cause of the 2017 Data Breach was that the company failed to apply a patch to a piece of software known as Apache Struts. I will talk more about this in the following chapters.

Equifax started building a new system known as CCMS (Consumer Care Management System) to replace ACIS in 2013.

Chapter Five –
The Cybersecurity Incident

During my time at Equifax, I had been involved in other security incidents. Equifax was and is an attractive target and we were constantly being probed and attacked—several thousand times a week, in fact.

The September 2017 incident was different, though.

Equifax Prepares for September 7th

On July 29th 2017, Equifax's security team deployed sixty-seven new digital certificates on an SSL[35] de-crypter linked to an intrusion prevention/detection system running in the data center. An intrusion prevention/detection system is designed to inspect traffic flowing across a network, to identify suspicious transmissions.

Encrypted traffic is network communication scrambled using a secret key. Only those who have the secret key can unscramble the data into a meaningful message. In order for an intrusion prevention/detection system to read and interrogate encrypted network traffic, it must have access to the secret key, and this is stored in a digital certificate.

---

[35] SSL - Secure Socket Layer - a commonly-used encryption technology implemented to create a secure link between a web server and a browser.

For the first time in over 12 months,[36] the Equifax security team had visibility into the encrypted communications that had been occurring between the ACIS dispute and disclosure web portal and the back-end databases and servers.

With this new-found visibility, the Equifax security team noticed some suspicious activity. The web server was receiving requests from a Chinese Internet Service Provider and the response going back contained more than ten megabytes of data and possibly image files. The Equifax security team ran an analysis tool (Moloch) and found persistent attempts to contact the ACIS web portal from this Chinese IP address since July 25th, 2017. The security team blocked the Chinese ISP and started to look deeper to see what was going on. The Equifax security team was unable to determine what had happened prior to July 29th, because the expired SSL certificates had effectively "hidden" the encrypted network traffic from inspection.

By the next day, the Equifax security team had performed a vulnerability analysis of the ACIS web server and found two common website vulnerabilities in the ACIS system: (1) a SQL Injection vulnerability that could allow an attacker to inject and retrieve database information; and (2) an Insecure Direct Object Reference vulnerability that could allow direct remote access to system without authentication or authorization.[37]

A second Internet Service Provider was identified as the source for requests with large data responses. This time, it was a German-owned

---

[36] It was later determined that the digital certificate on this SSL de-crypter had been expired for over twelve months.

[37] ACIS was tested for vulnerabilities in April 2017 and no un-remediated vulnerabilities were found.

ISP that had been leased to a Chinese provider. Given the type of personally identifiable data on this server, it was clearly time to bring the ACIS web portal offline until further analysis could be performed and the identified vulnerabilities addressed.

By this time, the Equifax Security team was in touch with the ACIS development and production support team. The Security team made a decision to bring the ACIS web portal offline and the team worked to make the necessary changes to bring the system offline. The ACIS web portal was shut down at 12:41 p.m. EDT on July 30th.

I had been out that Sunday and when I returned home, I noticed several missed calls from the CISO Susan Mauldin. I called her around 6.30 p.m. and found out that the security team had detected suspicious activity on the ACIS web portal and believed that the suspicious activity may be due to an exploit of a vulnerability in the Apache Struts software running on the ACIS web portal. The Equifax Security team needed help from the ACIS development team to do some research and asked for my help to get the right development focus to help the security team understand what might be happening.

The security team needed the ACIS developers to help gather files, determine file structures and layouts and only the developers and production support team had access to get the data needed by security to perform their research.

I joined a conference bridge that was in progress to see what help I could provide and we had some discussion about what type of message we should display on the website. The ACIS web portal had around 1 million visitors per month, so we knew we needed to have some message other than the standard "404 Not Found" message that would have been displayed when a consumer came to the site. The team decided we needed a "splash page" that would say the system was down for maintenance. This required coordination with another team that managed the web server and after a few hours of phone calls and discussions, we arrived at the right wordings and the splash page was installed. Now, if consumers came to the dispute website, they would be told it was down for system maintenance and to check back later.

A little later that evening I sent an email to my boss, Global CIO Dave Webb, simply stating that we had an ongoing security incident with the ACIS dispute and disclosure web portal and that we were working with Security to further investigate and had taken the ACIS web portal offline. CISO Susan Mauldin had already notified her boss Chief Legal Officer, John Kelley. Kelley was on vacation so Susan also notified his delegate.

On Monday morning (July 31st) I met with my boss, Dave Webb, and provided him an update, just a recap of what I knew from the Sunday discussions. I told him that I expected there may be some increase in calls to the call centers and perhaps some increased complaints to the CFPB portal or in social media. The dispute and disclosure web portal received about a million visitors each month. I also mentioned that if the site was down for a prolonged period, there could be some questions from the regulators.

Next, I joined an early morning call with various Security and IT personnel. It was time to declare a full-blown incident and so we set in place our standard incident response protocols. Every security incident was given a code name to allow the team to confidentially reference the incident. In this case, the incident project name was "Project Sierra."

Chapter Five: The Cybersecurity Incident

The security team was pretty sure by this stage that the hackers had gained access by leveraging a vulnerability in Apache Struts. Apache Struts is an open-source web application framework and widely used by the Fortune 100.

The Equifax security team working with the ACIS developers had now identified that a file had been inserted into the ACIS application. The forensic analysis would later determine that it was this file that was used by hackers to extract the information on 146 million consumers. So now, we were in serious security response mode. The security team continued to perform analysis and it became clear that we had a breach of sensitive, personally-identifiable information ("PII").

It would later be discovered that US-CERT (part of the Department of Homeland Security, responsible for analyzing and reducing cyber threats and vulnerabilities, disseminating cyber threat warning information, and coordinating incident response activities) had in fact sent a notification on March 8th, 2017 about a critical vulnerability in Apache Struts.

The Equifax Global Threat and Vulnerability Team within the Security function had reviewed that notification and a day later had issued an email about a critical patch needed to Apache Struts. I had received that email along with 429 other people. As a CIO, however, I was customarily copied on many notification emails. On an average day, I received 200-300 emails in my inbox.

The Equifax Security team ran a vulnerability scan on March 9th to identify any systems with a vulnerable version of Apache Struts. That scan did not identify any components utilizing an affected version of Apache Struts.

On that same Monday, the security team did a manual review for other instances of Apache Struts on other servers. They found a second dispute portal was also vulnerable. This server was taken offline for remediation. The security team was not aware of this server as it did not have an updated SSL certificate and therefore, network traffic to and from this reseller web portal was also not visible to intrusion prevention and detection devices.

Within two days, Equifax had engaged a major legal firm, King & Spalding, as their lead attorneys. King & Spalding operates in 160 countries with over 1,000 lawyers in twenty offices.

As is standard in these cases, King & Spalding hired Mandiant Consulting, a security consulting company, to perform a detailed forensic analysis. Having the law firm hire the forensics specialists is designed to ensure that all the work done by the specialists can be considered client-attorney work product and protected under the evidence rules followed in U.S. courts. Another standard protocol is to notify law enforcement, and on the same day, the FBI was notified of the breach and current status.

Several concurrent workstreams then commenced or continued over the next few weeks. Detailed forensic analysis was performed by Mandiant with assistance from the Equifax Security team and my team of ACIS developers and production support resources. Mandiant had requested and secured copies of the ACIS web server, database and logs for analysis. Over the next several weeks, they would be able to recreate the steps taken by the hackers to better understand what they did and how much data they were able to exfiltrate.

It was a challenging project for Mandiant to conduct this analysis. Mandiant had to take copies of several databases and tables and tie together a lot of information. There were only a few key employees who really understood how it all worked together and reporting and data extraction was challenging.

Mandiant also led an effort to identify areas that required remedial action. Their report was made public on September 19, 2017.

Whenever a company announces it has been breached, it is advertising to bad actors that it had (and may still have) weaknesses in its security posture. To help defend against this, best practice dictates that organizations harden their internet-facing attack surface to reduce the impact of this potential unwanted attention.

Hardening can include changing administrative passwords on databases and systems, implementing additional logging and monitoring, installing endpoint detection and response agents, accelerating file integrity monitoring deployment, improving privileged access controls, reconfiguring some network routes, and more. Many of these were included in Mandiant's report.

Meanwhile, at the corporate headquarters, other teams of lawyers and public relations experts were working on plans for the public notification, including press releases, a video, internal communications, and FAQs as well as plans to notify state and federal regulators under various breach notification rules.

Project Sparta

By about August 11th, it became clear that large amounts of dispute documents and other personally identifiable information had been accessed and exfiltrated. Interestingly, Equifax offered breach services to its business customers. These typically consisted of credit file monitoring and identity protection services that would be paid for by the breached company and offered free of charge to the impacted consumers for some period of time—generally one year.

Now, Equifax had to determine what it would provide to consumers impacted by this breach. The company decided to utilize an already existing product known as TrustedID Premier. The TrustedID Premier product included: copies of the consumer's Equifax credit report; the ability to lock the Equifax credit report; 3-Bureau credit monitoring of the consumer's Equifax, Experian and TransUnion credit reports; Internet scanning for the consumer's Social Security number; and identity theft insurance.

The challenge for Equifax was that this product was offered through a recently acquired subsidiary company, TrustedID which had not been fully integrated with the Equifax Global Consumer Services personal solutions business. Equifax typically serviced around 10-12 million consumers with their paid consumer products. Now, they had to be able to deal with tens of millions, many of whom would hit the website within a very short timeframe.

An IT team of about 50-60 IT employees and contractors set about architecting and building a web-based portal that would allow tens of millions of consumers to: (1) determine whether they had been impacted by the breach; and, (2) if impacted, sign up for the TrustedID Premier product for free. This project was code-named "Project Sparta." The Project Sparta team members were told they were working on a major breach deal for an unidentified customer.

Getting Started

Whether you are here for the first time or returning, please enter the information below and click **Continue**.

Last Name

Payne

Last 6 Digits of Social Security Number

Please enter the last 6 digits of your social security.

Continue

The New Era of Cybersecurity Breaches

The solution that the Project Sparta team designed consisted of:

- A web portal to provide information about the breach and allow consumers to input some basic personal information, thus confirming whether or not the consumer had been impacted by the breach.

- A front-end product registration workflow to allow a consumer to start the sign-up process for the TrustedID Premier product. The consumer would receive a notification email advising them that they would be notified when they could return to complete the enrolment process. The registration starts would go into a "bathtub" until they could be fulfilled.

- A "tap" that could be opened and closed to allow registration starts to flow through into the Equifax systems and enable or "turn on" the monitoring and identity protection services included in the TrustedID product. The idea was that the tap could be opened just enough to allow product enrollments to occur without bringing down various Equifax systems.

- An email response that was sent to the consumer when his or her registration was fulfilled, allowing them to complete the registration process and fully enroll in all the complimentary services.

Thank you

Based on the information you provided, our records indicate that your personal information was impacted by this incident.

What can I do?

For more information, visit the FAQ page.

The front-end system needed to be very scalable as potentially hundreds of millions of consumers might access the site when the public announcement was made.

Counting Down to Notification Day

By August 17th, the forensic work being performed by Mandiant had determined that large amounts of consumer data had been compromised. Mandiant met with some members of the Equifax Senior Leadership Team to discuss their findings. A week later, Mandiant was able to confirm significant volumes of PII had been accessed by the attackers.

On August 24th and 25th, CEO Richard Smith advised the Board of Directors of the breach and a full Board meeting was held on September 1st. Several Board meetings were held over the next week as a lead up to the public announcement on September 7th.

One of the challenges during a pre-notification period is how to keep a lid on the breach while at the same time making all the preparations for notification—hardening the systems, staffing up the call centers, completing the forensics, and developing the press and consumer notifications. The reality is that you need to continue to expand the circle of people in the trusted group who know what is happening; it is a balancing act. Each new person introduced into the war room must be briefed and advised of their responsibilities and the need to exercise utmost caution in talking about the breach.

Even so, news inevitably leaks out or smart people observe that something is afoot. This happened with two IT managers who "put two and two together" and worked out that the impacted company was Equifax. Based on this information, they are alleged to have sold shares and options prior to the breach.

At the time of writing, one has been found guilty and sentenced to house arrest, and the other has pleaded guilty and is awaiting sentencing. It is a somber lesson to everyone about the potential dangers of trading on insider information.

Another big challenge is preparing to deal with the inevitable customer inquiries that will occur when a breach is announced. Equifax typically only served a small number of consumers via call center agents, and so had to significantly scale up the contact call centers.

* * * *

And so, September 7th arrives. All the preparations are in place, press releases are ready, website ready to go live, and call centers are on standby. Thousands of hours of work had been performed by a relatively small number of people to prepare for the public notification.

Chapter Six –
Going Public: Notification and Response

Equifax Announces the Breach

Thursday September 7th, 2017 was the day chosen to "go public." Finally, the 4 p.m. Eastern hour came and various announcements were simultaneously launched to the media and employees.

The Equifax Press Release: September 7th, 2017:

Sep 07, 2017
No Evidence of Unauthorized Access to Core Consumer or Commercial Credit Reporting Databases
Company to Offer Free Identity Theft Protection and Credit File Monitoring to All U.S. Consumers

ATLANTA, Sept. 7, 2017 /PRNewswire/ -- Equifax Inc. (NYSE: EFX) today announced a cybersecurity incident potentially impacting approximately 143 million U.S. consumers. Criminals exploited a U.S. website application vulnerability to gain access to certain files. Based on the company's investigation, the unauthorized access occurred from mid-May through July 2017. The company has found no evidence of unauthorized activity on Equifax's core consumer or commercial credit reporting databases.

The information accessed primarily includes names, Social Security numbers, birth dates, addresses and, in some instances, driver's license numbers. In addition, credit card numbers for approximately 209,000 U.S. consumers, and certain dispute documents with personal identifying information for approximately 182,000 U.S. consumers, were accessed. As part of its investigation of this application vulnerability, Equifax also identified unauthorized access to limited personal information for certain UK and Canadian residents. Equifax will work with UK and Canadian regulators to determine appropriate next steps. The company has found no evidence that personal information of consumers in any other country has been impacted.

Equifax discovered the unauthorized access on July 29 of this year and acted immediately to stop the intrusion. The company promptly engaged a leading, independent cybersecurity firm that has been conducting a comprehensive forensic review to determine the scope of the intrusion, including the specific data impacted. Equifax also reported the criminal access to law enforcement and continues to work with authorities. While the company's investigation is substantially complete, it remains ongoing and is expected to be completed in the coming weeks.

"This is clearly a disappointing event for our company, and one that strikes at the heart of who we are and what we do. I apologize to consumers and our business customers for the concern and frustration this causes," said Chairman and Chief Executive Officer, Richard F. Smith. "We pride ourselves on being a leader in managing and protecting data, and we are conducting a thorough review of our overall security operations. We also are focused on consumer protection and have developed a comprehensive portfolio of services to support all U.S. consumers, regardless of whether they were impacted by this incident."

Equifax has established a dedicated website, www.equifaxsecurity2017.com, to help consumers determine if their information has been potentially impacted and to sign up for credit file monitoring and identity theft protection. The offering, called TrustedID Premier, includes 3-Bureau credit monitoring of Equifax, Experian and TransUnion credit reports; copies of Equifax credit reports; the ability to lock and unlock Equifax credit reports; identity theft insurance; and Internet scanning for Social Security numbers - all complimentary to U.S. consumers for one year. The website also provides additional information on steps consumers can take to protect their personal information. Equifax recommends that consumers with additional questions visit www.equifaxsecurity2017.com or contact a dedicated call center at 866-447-7559, which the company set up to assist consumers. The call center is open every day (including weekends) from 7:00 a.m. – 1:00 a.m. Eastern time.

In addition to the website, Equifax will send direct mail notices to consumers whose credit card numbers or dispute documents with personal identifying information were impacted. Equifax also is in the process of contacting U.S. state and federal regulators and has sent written notifications to all U.S. state attorneys general, which includes Equifax contact information for regulator inquiries.

Equifax has engaged a leading, independent cybersecurity firm to conduct an assessment and provide recommendations on steps that can be taken to help prevent this type of incident from happening again.

CEO Smith said, "I've told our entire team that our goal can't be simply to fix the problem and move on. Confronting cybersecurity risks is a daily fight. While we've made significant investments in data security, we recognize we must do more. And we will."

Equifax made it clear that they had "found no evidence of unauthorized activity on Equifax's core consumer or commercial reporting databases." In other words, the credit files on consumers had not been exposed.

The initial press release announced that the incident "potentially impacted approximately 143 million U.S. consumers" and criminals had accessed names, Social Security numbers, birth dates, addresses and in some instances driver's license numbers. Also accessed were credit card numbers and other information for a subset of consumers. Later, that number would be adjusted to 146 million consumers.

It only took about thirty minutes before headlines appeared on major news sites and television. By 6 p.m. Eastern time, it was a headline story on several channels. The media was using terms like "massive", "mega" and "giant" to demonstrate the comparative size of the breach.

Giant Equifax data breach: 143 million people could be affected –
CNN, September 8th

Massive Equifax data breach hits 143 million -
BBC News, September 8th

Also at this time, the consumer website was launched. Consumers, when they heard the news, could go to EquifaxSecurity2017.com, enter their information and find out if they had been impacted by the breach.

As well as the press release, Equifax posted a two-and-a-half-minute video statement by Chairman and CEO Richard Smith. In this statement, Richard Smith said: "We announced a cybersecurity incident that has impacted those who rely on us to protect their personal information...this is clearly a disappointing event and one that strikes at the heart of who we are and what we do...we are taking an unprecedented step of offering every U.S. consumer in the country a comprehensive package of identity theft protection and credit file monitoring at no cost...Equifax will not be defined by this incident, but rather by how we respond...." You can view the video here: https://www.youtube.com/watch?v=bh1gzJFVFLc.

Post-Breach Reaction

Security experts immediately criticized the company for launching a web portal that was not part of the Equifax domain. They claimed this was confusing. Here is just one example from nakedsecurity:[38]

"But Equifax didn't put their special breach site on something.equifax.com. Instead, they put it on www.equifaxsecurity2017.com a domain that happens to contain the word Equifax and looks like the sort of scam domain they probably spend a great deal of time and money telling customers and employees to ignore.

The name looks like a million similar domains that anyone could buy, and by using it, Equifax gave up its tremendous, inbuilt advantage with Google and levelled the playing field for anyone who wanted to create a scam site.

Naked Security's Mark Stockley knows, because he purchased two of them.

---

[38] Lisa Vaas, 09/22/17, Equifax has been sending customers to a fake phishing site for weeks, Nakedsecurity blog:
https://nakedsecurity.sophos.com/2017/09/22/equifax-has-been-sending-customers-to-a-fake-phishing-site-for-weeks/

In the course of investigating the breach on the morning after it was disclosed, he bought two domains that are exactly the same as www.equifaxsecurity2017.com but for a dash [equifax-security2017.com, equifaxsecurity-2017.com]. He owns, and controls, these look-alike domains, all for the princely sum of £30." (USD $41)

Some web browsers flagged the Equifax breach website as a dangerous phishing site and warned users not to access the site. This was not surprising given that the site was new and being flooded with requests.

A few weeks later someone noticed the Equifax team managing the Twitter feed had been tweeting "SecurityEquifax2017.com" instead of the correct site (EquifaxSecurity2017.com). A security researcher named Nick Sweeting had purchased the securityequifax2017.com domain and had set up a replica of the real site to demonstrate how easily someone could be fooled.

"I made the site because Equifax made a huge mistake by using a domain that doesn't have any trust attached to it [as opposed to hosting it on equifax.com]," Sweeting told The Verge. "It makes it ridiculously easy for scammers to come in and build clones—they can buy up dozens of domains, and typo-squat to get people to type in their info." Sweeting says no data will leave his page and that he "removed any risk of leaking data via network requests by redirecting them back to the user's own computer," so hopefully data entered on his site is relatively safe. Still, Equifax's team linked out to his page. That isn't reassuring"[39].

---

[39] Dani Deahl and Ashley Carman Sep 20, 2017. For weeks, Equifax customer service has been directing victims to a fake phishing site, The Verge, EDT
https://www.theverge.com/2017/9/20/16339612/equifax-tweet-wrong-website-phishing-identity-monitoring

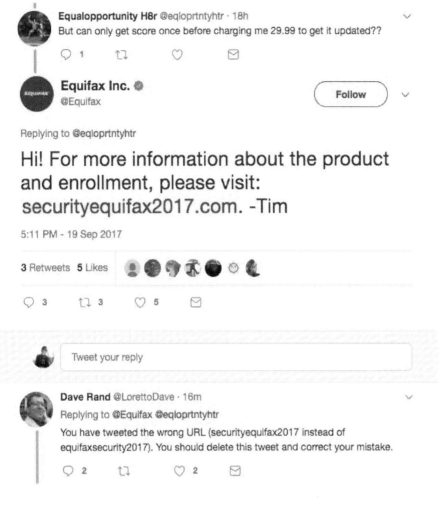

Equalopportunity H8r @eqloprtntyhtr · 18h

But can only get score once before charging me 29.99 to get it updated??

○ 1   ⟲   ♡   ✉

Equifax Inc. ✓
@Equifax

Follow

Replying to @eqloprtntyhtr

Hi! For more information about the product and enrollment, please visit: securityequifax2017.com. -Tim

5:11 PM - 19 Sep 2017

3 Retweets 5 Likes

○ 3   ⟲ 3   ♡ 5   ✉

Tweet your reply

Dave Rand @LorettoDave · 16m

Replying to @Equifax @eqloprtntyhtr

You have tweeted the wrong URL (securityequifax2017 instead of equifaxsecurity2017). You should delete this tweet and correct your mistake.

○ 2   ⟲   ♡ 2   ✉

The error was amplified by many different media outlets:

Equifax support team sent victims of breach to fake site -
US Today, September 21st

Equifax's big fat fail: How not to handle a data breach -
ZD Net, September 8th

Equifax Was Linking Potential Breach Victims on Twitter To a Scam Site - Forbes, September 21st

Someone Made a Fake Equifax Site. Then Equifax Linked to It - NY Times, September 20th

Sweeny took his fake website down on September 20th; however, it was reported that over 200,000 people had visited it. "My fake site is not malicious in any way. It loads over https, and I've disabled the eligibility form so that no information typed in gets sent anywhere or saved in any way," Sweeting said. "It's in everyone's interest to get Equifax to change this site to a reputable domain. I knew it would only cost me $15 to set up a site that would get people to notice, so I just did it. Their site is dangerously easy to impersonate. It only took me twenty minutes to build my clone. I can guarantee there are real malicious phishing versions already out there."[40] Equifax issued an apology for the confusion.

Around the same time, a security researcher found a vulnerability in the main Equifax website (equifax.com). Clicking on a link on the Equifax website redirected the user to a malicious URL that attempted to download a fake version of Adobe Flash Player. This was fixed by Equifax but added more fuel to the evolving public relations disaster around the breach and response.

Not surprisingly, with consumers on high alert about their data being breached, unscrupulous scammers started sending email scams to

---

[40] Tasnim Shamma, September 22, 2017, After Promoting Fake Site, Atlanta-based Equifax Deals With PR 'Nightmare', WABE website, https://www.wabe.org/after-promoting-fake-site-atlanta-based-equifax-deals-pr-nightmare/

consumers. Some of these were purported to have come from large banks like Bank of America and Wells Fargo but were fake messages luring consumers into clicking on links to steal their identify or download malware to their computer.

There was criticism about the irony of Equifax offering identity protection and credit monitoring when they were the cause of the breach. Further, in order to identify if a consumer had been impacted, they had to provide the last six digits of their social security number and name.

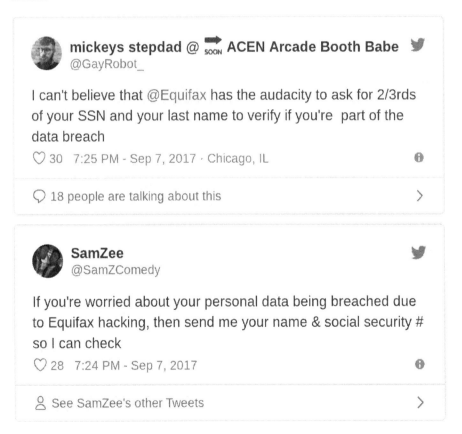

mickeys stepdad @ ACEN Arcade Booth Babe 🐦
@GayRobot_

I can't believe that @Equifax has the audacity to ask for 2/3rds of your SSN and your last name to verify if you're part of the data breach

♡ 30   7:25 PM - Sep 7, 2017 · Chicago, IL   ℹ

💬 18 people are talking about this   ›

SamZee 🐦
@SamZComedy

If you're worried about your personal data being breached due to Equifax hacking, then send me your name & social security # so I can check

♡ 28   7:24 PM - Sep 7, 2017   ℹ

👤 See SamZee's other Tweets   ›

The initial deployment of the website contained an error. It was quickly noticed and fixed but, in the meantime, consumers had come to the site, been told they **may have been** impacted and then when they returned, they were told they **were not impacted**. There was criticism about why Equifax was saying "may have" been impacted. From Krebs on Security:[41]

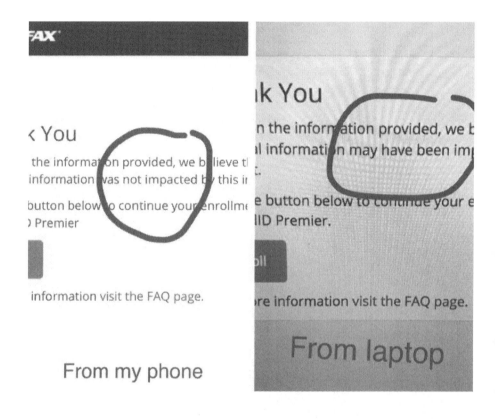

From my phone

From laptop

---

[41] Brian Krebs, 9/17/17, Equifax Breach Response Turns Dumpster Fire, Krebs on Security blog, https://krebsonsecurity.com/2017/09/equifax-breach-response-turns-dumpster-fire/

Answers seemed to be different depending on what device a consumer used to access the website. Some consumers found that entering gibberish data also reported that they had been impacted.

We tested Equifax's data breach checker — and it's basically useless - ZDNet, September 8th [42]

After a consumer had entered their name and the last six digits of their Social Security Number, they were told that they were either impacted or not impacted. The consumer could then register for the TrustedID product. Consumers would start the registration process and then would receive the email saying they would be contacted to complete the registration process in a few days.

"..the website that Equifax advertised as the place where concerned Americans could go to find out whether they were impacted by this breach — equifaxsecurity2017.com — is completely broken at best, and little more than a stalling tactic or sham at worst...In some cases, people visiting the site were told they were not affected, only to find they received a different answer when they checked the site with the same information on their mobile phones. Others (myself included) received not a yes or no answer to the question of whether we were impacted, but instead a message that credit monitoring services we were eligible for were not available and to check back later in the month. The site asked users to enter their last name and last six digits of their SSN, but at the prompting of a reader's comment I confirmed that just entering

---

[42] Zack Whittaker, September 8th, 2017, We tested Equifax's data breach checker — and it's basically useless, ZD Net https://www.zdnet.com/article/we-tested-equifax-data-breach-checker-it-is-basically-useless/

gibberish names and numbers produced the same result as the one I saw when I entered my real information: Come back on Sept. 13. [43]

Some consumers reported that the equifaxsecurity2017.com website, crashed several times in the days following the public announcement, according to Krebs on Security.

A standard Terms of Service appeared on the TrustedID website for when a consumer purchased the products, that stipulated that consumer would be bound by arbitration and limited their cause of action against Equifax. This should have been removed prior to going live but was not. There was a public outcry when this was discovered and Equifax removed the Terms of Service agreement and apologized for the error.

---

[43] Zack Whittaker, September 8th, 2017, We tested Equifax's data breach checker — and it's basically useless, ZD Net https://www.zdnet.com/article/we-tested-equifax-data-breach-checker-it-is-basically-useless/

Tim Hillard @timehillard · 8 Sep 2017

Beware @Equifax shameful offer of 1-year monitoring. Signing up means agreeing to binding arbitration for their error. #equifaxbreach

○ 34   ⊔⊐ 465   ♡ 344   ✉

The call centers and consumer contact channels (including email) were quickly overwhelmed. People started tweeting about this in the first few hours after the public announcement. When consumers did reach a call center representative, many complained that they could not answer basic questions about credit freezes and whether consumers had been impacted. Situations were cited where they provided callers with alternative numbers to call but the alternate number was a "triple-X hardcore service."[44]

Several security experts and consumer advocates noted that the response of offering credit monitoring was not sufficient. They recommended instead that consumers freeze their credit reports. A security freeze (or credit freeze) locks your credit report so that virtually no-one can perform a "hard inquiry" on your report. A hard inquiry is the term used when a lender accesses your credit report to check on your creditworthiness. A security freeze can be unlocked by a PIN code.

Senator Elizabeth Warren noted in her report on the breach: "Rather than acting solely to help consumers after the breach, Equifax instead used it as a moneymaking opportunity, attempting to profit off their own failures."[45] Since then, a federal law has mandated free credit freeze offerings at all of the big three credit reporting agencies.[46] This is something I would highly recommend to you and your family; you should freeze your credit report at each of the three credit reporting agencies.

---

[44] Ron Lieber , October 16, 2017, How to Protect Yourself After the Equifax Breach, The New York Times, https://www.nytimes.com/interactive/2017/your-money/equifax-data-breach-credit.html

[45] Elizabeth Warren, February 7, 2018, Bad Credit: Uncovering Equifax's Failure to Protect Americans' Personal Information, [hereafter referred to as "The Warren Report"] https://www.warren.senate.gov/files/documents/2018_2_7_%20Equifax_Report.pdf

[46] Free credit (security) freezes are available at Equifax, Experian and Transunion for free from September 21st, 2018. See: https://www.consumer.ftc.gov/blog/2018/09/free-credit-freezes-are-here

As problems continued with the breach website and Equifax continued to get hammered in the press, another disaster was brewing. This time, this was not of Equifax's making.

Hurricane Irma was heading towards the coast of Florida as a Category 5 storm. Equifax had one of its call centers in Florida and needed to close as the hurricane approached. By this time, the call centers were overwhelmed. They had long wait times, many in excess of an hour, and huge backlogs in email responses. When consumers were on hold, Equifax ran recorded messages offering various products for sale.

Consumers were complaining that they were receiving inconsistent or inaccurate information from call center agents. If a consumer wanted to place a fraud alert or request a security freeze, they were directed to call another number.

Here is an example of one frustrated consumer as reported by NBC News:[47]

Emily Lynch, a 38-year-old nurse from San Jose, California, had her identity stolen ten years ago. Having spent years since then polishing her score to a sterling "high 800's," she's eager to avoid a repeat.

"It was a total nightmare," she told NBC News. "It was a full-on investigation with the postal service inspector and all three credit bureaus. It took days and months dealing with that."

---

[47] Ben Popken, 9/13/17, Consumer Equifax Fallout: FTC Launches Probe, Websites and Phones Jammed With Angry Consumers, NBC News, https://www.nbcnews.com/business/consumer/equifax-melts-down-under-surge-angry-consumers-n800991

The New Era of Cybersecurity Breaches

But when she filed a credit freeze with Equifax after the recent breach was announced, the website said it was unable to process her request. When she called the automated credit freeze phone line, she was told that she had already had a credit freeze placed on her report. She never got a PIN code though, and now has no way of unlocking it.

She says when she called customer service, they recommended she try "tomorrow" because it was a "computer glitch." When she asked how she would get a PIN, she says the customer service representative told her, "I don't know."

Lynch was stunned.

"This is one of the top three credit agencies, you're hiring people to work the phone for a huge mistake, probably one of the largest ever for this industry, and you're hiring people who have no idea what the answers are?" she said.

Many consumers turned to other providers for additional identity protection services. Companies like LifeLock and Credit Karma were among those who saw a rise in business. LifeLock reported a tenfold increase in business in the month after the breach was announced. These companies gained their data from Equifax and so Equifax benefited from the use of these services.

The FTC announced that it was investigating Equifax on September 14th. This was considered unusual as the FTC does not normally announce open or ongoing investigations.

On September 13th, Equifax posted some additional data about the breach:

> **Updated information on US website application vulnerability.**
> *"Equifax has been intensely investigating the scope of the intrusion with the assistance of a leading, independent cyber security firm to determine what information was accessed and who has been impacted. We know that criminals exploited a US website application vulnerability. The vulnerability was Apache Struts CVE-2017-5638. We continue to work with law enforcement as part of a criminal investigation, and have shared indicators of compromise with law enforcement."*

This is a good example of the balance that must be managed during a crisis—the need to provide information, balanced against sharing information that may not be complete or that just gives rise to more questions. The Apache Foundation responded and stated that the breach "was due to [Equifax's] failure to install the security updates provided in a timely manner."[48]

Executive Departures

On September 15th, Equifax acknowledged the Apache Struts prior alert and announced that Global CIO Dave Webb and CSO Susan Mauldin were retiring immediately. The press release also acknowledged issues with Equifax breach response and noted some of the improvements it had made.

---

[48] Elizabeth Weise and Nathan Bomey, 9/14/17, Equifax had patch 2 months before hack and didn't install it, security group says, The Record.com, https://www.therecord.com/news-story/7556494-equifax-had-patch-2-months-before-hack-and-didn-t-install-it-security-group-says/

The New Era of Cybersecurity Breaches

Equifax Releases Details on Cybersecurity Incident, Announces Personnel Changes
Sep 15, 2017

ATLANTA, Sept. 15, 2017 /PRNewswire/ -- As part of the company's ongoing review of the cybersecurity incident announced September 7, 2017, Equifax Inc. (NYSE: EFX) today made personnel changes and released additional information regarding its preliminary findings about the incident.

The company announced that the Chief Information Officer and Chief Security Officer are retiring. Mark Rohrwasser has been appointed interim Chief Information Officer. Mr. Rohrwasser joined Equifax in 2016 and has led Equifax's International IT operations since that time. Russ Ayres has been appointed interim Chief Security Officer. Mr. Ayres most recently served as a Vice President in the IT organization at Equifax. He will report directly to the Chief Information Officer. The personnel changes are effective immediately.

Equifax's internal investigation of this incident is still ongoing and the company continues to work closely with the FBI in its investigation.

Specific Details of Incident:

- *On July 29th, 2017, Equifax's Security team observed suspicious network traffic associated with its U.S. online dispute portal web application. In response, the Security team investigated and blocked the suspicious traffic that was identified.*
- *The Security team continued to monitor network traffic and observed additional suspicious activity on July 30th, 2017. In response, the company took offline the affected web application that day.*
- *The company's internal review of the incident continued. Upon discovering a vulnerability in the Apache Struts web application framework as the initial attack vector, Equifax patched the affected web application before bringing it back online.*
- *On August 2nd, 2017, Equifax contacted a leading, independent cybersecurity firm, Mandiant, to assist in conducting a privileged, comprehensive forensic review to determine the scope of the intrusion, including the specific data impacted.*
- *Over several weeks, Mandiant analyzed available forensic data to identify unauthorized activity on the network.*
- *The incident potentially impacts personal information relating to 143 million U.S. consumers – primarily names, Social Security numbers, birth dates, addresses and, in some instances, driver's license numbers.*
  - *In addition, credit card numbers for approximately 209,000 U.S. consumers, and certain dispute documents with personal identifying information for approximately 182,000 U.S. consumers, were accessed.*
  - *Equifax also identified unauthorized access to limited personal information for certain U.K. and Canadian*

> *residents and is working with regulators in those countries.*
> - *With respect to the company's security posture, Equifax has taken short-term remediation steps, and Equifax continues to implement and accelerate long-term security improvements.*

Questions Regarding Apache Struts:

- *The attack vector used in this incident occurred through a vulnerability in Apache Struts (CVE-2017-5638), an open-source application framework that supports the Equifax online dispute portal web application.*
- *Based on the company's investigation, Equifax believes the unauthorized accesses to certain files containing personal information occurred from May 13 through July 30th, 2017.*
- *The particular vulnerability in Apache Struts was identified and disclosed by U.S. CERT in early March 2017.*
- *Equifax's Security organization was aware of this vulnerability at that time, and took efforts to identify and to patch any vulnerable systems in the company's IT infrastructure.*
- *While Equifax fully understands the intense focus on patching efforts, the company's review of the facts is still ongoing. The company will release additional information when available.*

Overview of Consumer Support Response and Recent Developments

The company is fully committed to proactively supporting consumers who may have been impacted by the cybersecurity incident. A timeline of our response includes:
- *The company worked diligently with Mandiant to determine what information was accessed and identify the potentially*

impacted consumers in order to make an appropriate public disclosure of the incident.

- *As soon as the company understood the potentially impacted population, a comprehensive support package was rolled out to consumers on September 7, 2017.*
- *Equifax took the following steps:*
  - *Created a dedicated website where consumers could understand whether they were impacted, find out more information about the incident and learn how to protect themselves.*
  - *The company offered free credit file monitoring and identity theft protection to all U.S. consumers, regardless of whether they were definitively impacted.*
    - *TrustedID Premier includes 3-Bureau credit monitoring of Equifax, Experian, and TransUnion credit reports; copies of Equifax credit reports; the ability to lock and unlock Equifax credit reports; identity theft insurance; and Internet scanning for Social Security numbers.*
  - *The company has also set up a dedicated call center to assist consumers with questions and signing up for the free offering and has continued to ramp up the call center to reduce wait times.*
- *Equifax also provided written notification to all U.S. State Attorneys General and contacted other federal regulators.*
- *Since the announcement, Equifax has taken additional actions including:*
  - *Providing a more prominent and clear link from the main www.equifax.com website to the cybersecurity incident website www.equifaxsecurity2017.com, so that*

consumers can quickly and easily find the information they need.

- *Tripling the call center team and continuing to add agents, despite facing some difficulty due to Hurricane Irma.*
- *Resolving issues with the impact look-up tool.*
- *Addressing confusion concerning the arbitration and class-action waiver clauses included in the Terms of Use applicable to the product:*
  - *The company never intended for these clauses to apply to this cybersecurity incident.*
  - *Because of consumer concern, the company clarified that those clauses do not apply to this cybersecurity incident or to the complimentary TrustedID Premier offering.*
  - *The company clarified that the clauses will not apply to consumers who signed up before the language was removed.*
- *Clarifying that no credit card information is required to sign up for the product and that consumers will not be automatically enrolled or charged after the conclusion of the complimentary year.*
- *Making changes to address consumer concerns regarding security freezes:*
  - *The company clarified that consumers placing a security freeze will be provided a randomly generated PIN.*
  - *The company continues to work on technical difficulties related to the high volume of security freeze requests.*

- *Consumers who paid for a security freeze starting at 5pm EST on September 7, 2017 will receive a refund.*
- *The company agreed to waive fees for removing and placing security freezes through November 21ˢᵗ, 2017.*

On the day of the public announcement, the Equifax stock price was $143. The stock price dropped to a low of $85, wiping out $6 billion in market capitalization. Eighteen months later—at the time of writing this book—the stock price has rebounded to around $126 (April 2019). This is in line with the general trend observed in other large data breaches. There is little long-term impact on stock prices for companies suffering data breaches.

On September 26ᵗʰ, Equifax announced that the CEO Richard Smith was retiring effective immediately and that Paulino Barros was stepping in as the Interim CEO while the Board sought a permanent replacement.

Richard Smith retired with his full pension, which was valued at $18.4 million as of the end of 2016. He agreed to forego his 2017 bonus or severance payment. At the time of his retirement, he held stock in Equifax, valued at $24 million.[49] Various reports claimed he retired with $90 million. Three senior executives had now retired from Equifax— CEO Richard Smith, CIO David Webb and CISO Susan Mauldin.

In the weeks following the announcement, various House and Senate committees announced that they would hold hearings into the details of the Equifax Breach. These initial hearings were scheduled for the first

---

[49] He had sold $19 million of stocks earlier in 2017.

week of October, and CEO Richard Smith had agreed to appear. He would continue to appear although he was now the former Chairman and CEO of Equifax. The schedule of hearings included appearances before the following committees:

- House Energy and Commerce Committee
- Senate Banking Committee
- Senate Judiciary Subcommittee on Privacy
- House Financial Services Committee.

On September 29th, Paulino Barros—the new Interim CEO—published an Op Ed in the Wall Street Journal. Barros apologized:

"People across the country and around the world, including our friends and family members, put their trust in our company. We didn't live up to expectations."[50]

He commented that Equifax compounded the problem of being hacked by its response that provided "insufficient support for consumers". He also talked about the new approach for protecting consumer data, allowing "consumers the power to protect and control access to their personal credit data" and committed to have this solution available by 31st January 2018. The free credit freeze window and the ability to sign up for the TrustedID free product were extended to 31st January 2018.

---

[50] Paulino do Rego Barros Jr. September 27, 2017, On Behalf of Equifax, I'm Sorry, OpEd in The Wall Street Journal, https://www.wsj.com/articles/on-behalf-of-equifax-im-sorry-1506547253

"We have to see this breach as a turning point—not just for Equifax, but for everyone interested in protecting personal data. Consumers need the power to control access to personal data.
Critics will say we are late to the party. But we have been studying and developing a potential solution for some time, as have others. Now it is time to act."[51]

On Monday, October 2nd, I was terminated from Equifax.

The next day, Tuesday October 3rd, I grabbed a coffee and sat in front of my TV to watch Former CEO Richard Smith appear before the House Energy and Commerce Committee, Subcommittee on Digital Commerce and Consumer Protection. Committee Chair Mr. Latta opened the proceedings:

"Good morning. The Subcommittee on Digital Commerce and Consumer Protection will come to order. The chair now recognizes himself for five minutes for an opening statement.

Good morning. Today we are here to get the facts to learn what happened at Equifax that led to the personal information of over 143 million Americans' information being stolen. Americans need to know what Equifax is doing to fix the problem and help individuals that are impacted. We must find out what happened. The public deserves to know what happened and what steps are being taken to protect their sensitive data going forward. Today's hearing needs to shed some much-needed information and light on this breach. We have received assurances from Equifax that Mr. Smith can speak for the company on concrete remediation steps that the company took in the aftermath to secure its

---

[51] Ibid

computer systems to protect the affected U.S. customers as well as what happened when he was Chief Executive... "[52]

Minority ranking member Ms. Schakowsky then gave her opening statement that included:

"The Equifax data breach was massive in scale. I would call it shocking, but is it really? We have these underregulated, private, for-profit credit reporting agencies collecting detailed personal and financial information about American consumers. It is a treasure trove for hackers... Because consumers don't have a choice, we can't trust credit reporting agencies to self-regulate... When it comes to information security, you are at the mercy of whatever Equifax decides is right and once your information is compromised, the damage is ongoing... From media reports and the subcommittee's meeting with Equifax officials after the breach, it is clear to me that the company lacked appropriate policies and practices around data security....The response to the breach was its own debacle...Equifax deserves to be shamed in this hearing, but we should also ask what Congress has done or failed to do to stop data breaches from occurring and what Equifax plans to do..."

Smith started by reading a prepared summary. He had previously submitted a written testimony to the Committee.

---

[52] House of Representatives, Subcommittee on Digital Commerce and Consumer Protection, Committee on Energy and Commerce, October 3rd, 2017, OVERSIGHT OF THE EQUIFAX DATA BREACH: ANSWERS FOR CONSUMERS Preliminary Transcript

He stated:

"My name is Rick Smith and for the last twelve years, I have had the honor of being the CEO and chairman of Equifax... I am here today to explain to you and the American people how criminal hackers were able to steal personal information on over 145 million Americans from our servers, and, as importantly, to discuss with you today what our company's response was to that criminal hack. The criminal hack happened on my watch and as CEO, I am ultimately responsible and I take full responsibility. I am here today to say to each and every person affected by this breach, I am truly and deeply sorry for what happened...

"Americans have a right to know how this happened and I am prepared to testify today about what I have learned and what I did about this incident in my role as CEO and as Chairman of the Board, and also what I know about the incident as a result of being briefed by the company's investigation which is ongoing.

*"We know now that this criminal attack was made possible because of a combination of **human error and technological error [emphasis added]**. The human error involved the failure to apply a software patch to our dispute portal in March of 2017. The technological error involved a scanner which failed to detect that vulnerability on that particular portal. Both errors have since been addressed."*

As I listened to this statement, I heard the mention of a human error as the failure to apply a software patch.

Mr. Smith then went on to speak about the challenges of the Equifax response, again apologizing and explaining that steps had been taken to address the issues. He then announced a new solution that Equifax was building to help protect consumers:

"At my direction, the company offered a broad package of services to all Americans. In addition, we developed a new service available on January 31st, 2018 that will give all consumers the power to control access to their credit data by allowing them to lock and unlock their credit files when they want and they can do that for free for life. Putting the power to control access to credit data in the hands of the American consumer is a step forward..."

Work on the "Lock and Alert" solution referred to by Mr. Smith had started while I was still at Equifax. This was an interesting solution designed to give consumers control over their credit report directly from their phone or personal device.

After Mr. Smith's testimony, the representatives then started with questioning. In the question and answer session, the following comments were made:

The Chairman: *"If I could, the human error piece you reference is that they didn't know that that particular software was running on your system, Apache Struts was running? Because that is what needed patching, right?"*

Mr. Smith: *"Congressman, great question, if I may clarify."*

The Chairman: *"Yes, please."*

Mr. Smith: *"The human error was the individual who is responsible for communicating in the organization to apply the patch did not."*

The Chairman: *"So, does that mean that that individual knew that the software was there and it needed to be patched and did not communicate that to the team that does the patching? Is that the heart of the issue here?"*

Mr. Smith. *"That is my understanding, Sir."*

A little later in the questioning, there were more questions about the patching process:

Mr. Harper: *"All right. In your testimony you indicate that the security department ran scans in March for the vulnerability but failed to identify it. Can you explain how this is possible and why was there never any confirmation of anybody coming back and checking to see it was being used, that the software was even being used? Was there no one coming in to verify that? Do you have any outside person prior to the ones that you hired to look at this?*

Mr. Smith: *"Congressman, we get notifications routinely, the IT team and security team do, to apply applications. This individual as I mentioned earlier did not communicate to the right level to apply the patch. The follow-up was as you mentioned—"*

Mr. Harper: *"You said 'this individual'?"*

Mr. Smith: *"Yes."*

Mr. Harper: *"So you had one person responsible for this?"*

Mr. Smith: *"There is an owner of the patch process. There is a communication that comes out from security. It is a broad-based* *communication. Once they receive notification from a software company, or in this case DHS, they notify appropriate people. Then an individual who owns the patch process cascades that communication."*

Richard Smith would testify another five times that week to both House and Senate committees. The questions and responses would be similar, as was the outrage and frustration voiced by representatives and senators. The hearings received a lot of coverage in the news media.

6 Fresh Horrors from the Equifax CEO's Congressional Hearing - Wired Magazine[53]

Lawmakers Slam Equifax Ex-CEO Over Hack - The Wall Street Journal[54]

Former Equifax CEO blames breach on a single person who failed to deploy patch - The Verge[55]

---

[53] ILY HAY NEWMAN,10/3/17, 6 FRESH HORRORS FROM THE EQUIFAX CEO'S CONGRESSIONAL HEARING, Wired Magazine, https://www.wired.com/story/equifax-ceo-congress-testimony/

[54] AnnaMaria Andriotis, Michael Rapoport and Christina Rexrode, October 3rd, 2017, Lawmakers Slam Equifax Ex-CEO Over Hack, The Wall Street Journal, https://www.wsj.com/articles/lawmakers-slam-equifax-ex-ceo-over-hack-1507051747

[55] Russell Brandom, October 3rd, 2017, Former Equifax CEO blames breach on a single person who failed to deploy patch, The Verge, https://www.theverge.com/2017/10/3/16410806/equifax-ceo-blame-breach-patch-congress-testimony

My name was not mentioned in any of the testimony. In the Senate Judiciary Committee hearing, Senator Al Franken questioned Smith more about the human error:[56]

Senator Franken: *"Thank you, Mr. Chairman. Mr. Smith, you were talking about human error. I want to be clear about something. In your written testimony, you referenced that sophisticated cyber criminals who had been behind attacks on a long list of countries and agencies, including now yours, but I understand numerous other entities were provided with the same US-CERT alert that Equifax was. For those entities, the vulnerability was assessed and patched. In some cases, within hours and at very little cost. Mr. Smith, this was not a novel vulnerability with a novel solution. Would you agree?"*

Mr. Smith: *"Guess, I would."*

Senator Franken: *"Yesterday, you told Representative Walden that the human error was the individual who was responsible for communicating to the organization to apply the patch did not... does that mean the individual knew that the software was there, that it needed to be patched, and did not communicate that to the team, that does the patching? Is that the heart of the issue here, and you confirm that was the case. You just said that was the same thing, right?"*

Mr. Smith: *"Verification, if I may. I'm not certain the individual responsible for indicating the patch knew that the software was deployed. He was responsible for communicating to his team to look for the software if the software existed, patch the software."*

---

[56] C-SPAN, October 4th, 2017, Senate Judiciary Committee Hearing on Equifax Data Breach, transcript and video, https://www.c-span.org/video/?434977-2/senate-judiciary-committee-hearing-equifax-data-breach

Senator Franken: *"Still, it is an individual. I guess my question is why is the security of 145 million Americans' personal information all in the hands of one guy? Why is it all up to Gus? When did you, knowing the seriousness of these, put it in the hands of one guy to screw up?"*

Mr. Smith: *"This one guy was responsible for the patching process. He had a team underneath him. He did not communicate that the closed loop process was followed."*

Senator Franken: *"That does not change that it was up to one guy. And you said that this was human error, and that this was one guy."*

Mr. Smith: *"As I mentioned in my comments, it was followed up by technology. We deployed a scanner on March 15 that was looking for vulnerabilities, and it did not find it either."*

So now, the un-named individual has a name—"Gus"!

Some observers were critical of the company blaming this on a single individual.

Failure Has a Name at Equifax. Al Franken Says It's 'Gus'- Bloomberg News[57]

---

[57] Elizabeth Dexheimer and Jennifer Surane, October 4th, 2017, Failure Has a Name at Equifax. Al Franken Says It's 'Gus', Bloomberg News, https://www.bloomberg.com/news/articles/2017-10-04/failure-has-a-name-at-equifax-al-franken-says-it-s-gus

Former CEO of Equifax blames a single IT worker for massive hack of over 145 million Americans' financial histories - DailyMail[58]

It was an uneasy feeling knowing that you were the person that Smith was referring to, yet no one (except me) knew that. I started to wonder about my future job prospects. How would my association with Equifax be viewed by prospective employers? I reached out to some of my friends in the industry and was heartened when most said that "most companies would want to hire someone who has lived through this breach—at least you know what to do and what not to do."

$$* * * *$$

The previous ten weeks had been a whirlwind of activity and emotion. Equifax had suffered one of the worst data breaches of our time. Hackers had gained access to 146 million American consumers' data because a web server had remained unpatched for four months.

How do you recover from a major breach and a challenging response process? How do you regain trust and rebuild your reputation? What are the longer-range impacts? Clearly, it is a challenging time.

---

[58] IAIN BURNS FOR MAILONLINE, October 6th, 2017, Former CEO of Equifax blames a single IT worker for massive hack of over 145 million Americans' financial histories, DailyMail.com, https://www.dailymail.co.uk/news/article-4955972/Former-Equifax-CEO-blames-one-guy-major-hack.html

Chapter Seven –
Challenging Times

Investigations and Lawsuits

In the immediate weeks following the September 7, 2017, Data Breach announcement by Equifax, several federal and state agencies, and congressional committees announced that they were launching investigations into how the breach occurred and the Equifax response.

Within days of the public announcement, several class action lawsuits were filed in Federal courts throughout the country. Typically, these suits are filed against the company as the defendant but in one case, the plaintiff identified eleven Equifax employees by name as co-defendants. I was one of those eleven employees. At that time, no other reports had been issued about the breach and so I assumed that the plaintiff's lawyer had found our names from a LinkedIn search and had included us as co-defendants based on the job descriptions, we had listed on our LinkedIn profiles.

The Federal Trade Commission took the unusual step of announcing on September 14th that it was investigating the data breach. Normally, the FTC does not announce details of ongoing investigations.

"The FTC typically does not comment on ongoing investigations," said Peter Kaplan, the agency's acting director of public affairs. "However, in light of the intense public interest and the potential impact of this

matter, I can confirm that FTC staff is investigating the Equifax data breach."[59]

The Consumer Financial Protection Bureau also announced it was looking into Equifax's response to the breach.

On September 18th, *Bloomberg News* reported that the Department of Justice was conducting an investigation into the share trading of three senior executives—Chief Financial Officer, John Gamble; President of U.S. Information Solutions, Trey Loughran; and President of Workforce Solutions, Rudy Ploder. The three senior executives sold almost $2 million worth of stock, days after the company learned of the breach.[60]

After I left in early October 2017, the Equifax Data Breach story continued to unfold. In early November 2017, another round of hearings was held, more broadly, on data breaches. The Senate Commerce Committee held a hearing on data breaches and ways to further secure the personal information of consumers. Witnesses included Mr. Richard Smith (Former CEO) and Mr. Paulino Barros (current CEO of Equifax). Also on the panel were Melissa Meyers (former CEO of Yahoo!), Karen Zacharia, Deputy General Counsel and Chief Privacy Officer, Verizon Communications and, Todd Wilkinson, President and CEO, Entrust Datacard.

---

[59] By Brian Fung and Hamza Shaban, September 14th, 2017, The FTC is investigating the Equifax breach. Here's why that's a big deal, The Washington Post, https://www.washingtonpost.com/news/the-switch/wp/2017/09/14/the-ftc-confirms-its-investigating-the-equifax-breach-adding-to-a-chorus-of-official-criticism/?utm_term=.2f637639e716

[60] The sale of stock took place on August 1st, 2017, three days after Equifax first identified the breach

I was also interviewed by lawyers hired by the Equifax Board of Directors to investigate the stock sales by the three senior executives. The committee's six-page report on its findings was released on November 3rd and concluded that none of the executives had known about the security breach when they asked to clear their stock trades. The committee also concluded that the sales were properly approved, followed company policy, and weren't insider trading[61].

The committee interviewed dozens of people and reviewed more than 55,000 emails, text messages, phone logs and other documents. "The conclusion that the Company executives in question traded appropriately is an extremely important finding and very reassuring," said Mark Feidler, Equifax's Non-Executive Chairman.

Lock and Alert Delivered

On January 31st, 2018 Equifax launched its Lock and Alert Product as promised by Interim CEO Paulino Barros in the November Congressional hearings. Here is the "Lock and Alert" press release issued on January 31st, 2018:

January 31, 2018
***Equifax Launches Lock & Alert*[TM]**
Free-for-life service offers consumers the ability to lock and unlock their Equifax® credit report

---

[61] The report is available at: https://investor.equifax.com/news-and-events/news/2017/11-03-2017-124511096

The New Era of Cybersecurity Breaches

ATLANTA, January 31, 2018 –*Equifax (NYSE: EFX), a global information solutions provider, today announced the availability of Lock & Alert, a new service that enables consumers to quickly lock and unlock their Equifax credit report using a computer or app downloaded on their mobile device from either the Apple® App Store or Google Play™ Store.*

U.S. consumers who are 18 years or older and have an Equifax credit report may enroll in this service, which is available for free, for life. Once a consumer has enrolled in the service, Equifax will send an alert each time he or she locks or unlocks their Equifax credit report.

"Regaining consumer trust and ensuring them that we are listening is one of our highest priorities" said Paulino do Rego Barros, Jr., Interim CEO, Equifax. "Today, we are delivering on the commitment we announced on Sept. 27, 2017, to provide a service that allows consumers to help control access to their personal Equifax credit report in an easy and convenient way.

"Not only does Lock & Alert empower consumers to help restrict certain access to their Equifax credit report, which may help better protect against unauthorized access and identity theft, it also gives them the ability to lock and unlock their report through a convenient app on their mobile device," added Barros.

The new Lock & Alert service is similar to a security freeze as it restricts certain access to a consumer's Equifax credit report for purposes of opening new credit, but Lock & Alert uses usernames and passwords, as well as mobile app technology. It also has no associated fees.

If a consumer enrolls in Lock & Alert, and later decides to apply for a loan or purchase a vehicle, he or she will be able to quickly unlock their Equifax credit report to allow a lender access. Once the credit check is complete, the consumer is able to quickly re-lock their Equifax credit report using the app on his or her mobile device.

"The consumer-empowerment approach that is offered through Lock & Alert is what people have come to expect," said Barros. "I'm pleased we are able to deliver on a promise we committed to, and empower individuals with another way to restrict certain access to their Equifax credit reports."

Lock & Alert is an Equifax-only service, and consumers should contact the other two major credit bureaus should they wish to lock or freeze their credit reports with those bureaus.

The "Lock and Alert" product received a lukewarm reaction in the media. There were some initial registration issues which didn't help build confidence. Most consumer advocates were now recommending consumers freeze their credit reports rather than use the lock and alert product. Equifax also extended the free credit freeze options through June 2018.[62]

"The Equifax website talks about the convenience of Lock & Alert, but some have found it a challenge to get started. When NBC News tried to sign up, we got an error message: "Please give us a call. We cannot complete your registration at this time."

---

[62] Congress would later require all credit reporting agencies to provide free credit freezes.

"Equifax customer care said everything was OK, but when we tried to sign on, we received another error message: "We are experiencing technical issues. Please try again later." After several more failed attempts, we made another call to customer service and were told to expect an email in 24-48 hours with a link to log in. That email never arrived. When we later logged on again, we were able to gain access.

"I think it's fair to say, as with any service, we did have some initial operational issues shortly after the launch," Nancy Bistritz-Balkan, Equifax's Director of Public Relations & Communications, told NBC News. "But our team has been working around the clock to document the issues and address it appropriately."[63]

Bad Credit - The Warren Report

In February 2018, Senator Elizabeth Warren released a report: "Bad Credit: Uncovering Equifax's Failure to Protect Americans' Personal Information."[64]

The report was compiled following a five-month investigation by Warren's office into the Equifax breach and response, including a review of documents, and interviews with consultants and experts. The Warren report concluded:

---

[63] Herb Weisbaum, Feb. 8, 2018, After mega hack, Equifax launches free 'Lock & Alert' service — with mixed results, NBC News, https://www.nbcnews.com/business/consumer/after-mega-hack-equifax-launches-free-lock-alert-service-mixed-n845941

[64] "The Warren Report" (see page 94 footnote)

- Equifax set up a flawed system to prevent and mitigate data security problems;
- Equifax ignored numerous warnings of risks to sensitive data;
- Equifax failed to notify consumers, investors and regulators about the breach in a timely and appropriate fashion;
- Equifax took advantage of federal contracting loopholes and failed to adequately protect sensitive IRS taxpayer data;
- Equifax assistance and information provided to consumers following the breach was inadequate;
- Federal legislation is necessary to prevent and respond to future breaches.

The Warren Report identified six areas where Equifax's cybersecurity measures were particularly deficient:

1. **Faulty Patch Management Procedures** - "Equifax let numerous vulnerabilities sit un-patched for months at a time, leaving weaknesses through which hackers could gain access."

2. **Feeble Monitoring of Endpoint and Email Security** - "Equifax failed to adopt strict endpoint and email security measures to secure each endpoint on the network."

3. **Exposure of Sensitive Information** - Equifax stored and "retained sensitive consumer information on easily accessible systems" rather than segregating the most sensitive information into locations designed to limit access and maximize security.

4. **Weak Network Segmentation** - Equifax "failed to put security measures in place that would prevent hackers from jumping

from insecure, Internet-facing systems to back-end databases that contain more valuable data...Equifax's network segmentation measures failed to keep hackers from accessing consumer information..."

5. **Inadequate Credentialing** - "After gaining access to Equifax systems, hackers then acquired user credentials - a username and password - and accessed a huge quantity of sensitive information using just those credentials."

6. **Inadequate Logging** - "Equifax neglected the use of robust logging techniques that could have allowed the company to expel the hackers from their systems and limited the size and scope of the data breach. Equifax allowed hackers to continuously access sensitive data for over seventy-five days, in part because the company failed to adopt effective logging techniques and other security measures."

A New Team at Equifax

In February 2018, Equifax appointed Jamil Farshchi as its new Chief Information Security Officer (CISO). "Farshchi has some experience cleaning up data breach disasters. He comes to Equifax from Home Depot, where Farshchi was brought on after the retailer disclosed that its payment systems were breached in a malware attack in April 2014."[65]

---

[65]Natalie Gagliordi, Equifax hires Home Depot's CISO to lead security turnaround, ZD Net, https://www.zdnet.com/article/equifax-hires-home-depots-ciso-to-lead-security-turnaround/

In March 2018, Equifax announced that they were hiring a new CEO, Mark Begor. Begor was previously at a private equity firm Warburg Pincus, but most of his career was at General Electric. He was also on the board of directors for FICO.

Begor's initial pay package was $20 million ($1.5 million base + $1.5 million bonus + $17 sign on stock grants). Begor stated: "We didn't have the right defenses in place, but we are investing in the business to protect this from ever happening again," Begor said. "We are a public trust in many regards and we need to work to earn that trust back."[66]

In June, Equifax hired a new Chief Technology Officer, Bryson Koehler. Bryson was the former Chief Technology Officer at IBM Watson and Cloud Platform. The Equifax announcement emphasized his "innovative use of technology" which meant driving Equifax to utilize more cloud technologies:

"Bryson is known for his deep technical and cloud skills, consistent, focused, and strong performance within the industry, and for being a creative problem solver who has achieved business goals by leveraging the innovative use of technology. This is paramount to our future success as we advance our technology capabilities, and enhance data security and the speed, simplicity, and reliability of our products. We are thrilled to have a leader of Bryson's caliber joining Equifax at such a pivotal time in our history."[67]

---

[66] KEN SWEET, March 28th, 2018, Equifax Hires Financial Executive Mark Begor as New CEO, U.S. News, https://www.usnews.com/news/business/articles/2018-03-28/equifax-names-mark-begor-as-its-ceo
[67] Equifax press release, June 14th, 2018:
https://investor.equifax.com/news-and-events/news/2018/06-14-2018-140025366

Settlements and Reports

On June 25th, 2018, Equifax entered into a Consent Order with eight state banking regulators. Equifax agreed to improve oversight of its information security program within ninety days by, among other things, reviewing and approving information technology and information security policies. The Consent Order also required Equifax to improve the standards and controls for patch management.

Senators Elizabeth Warren and Ron Wyden and Representatives Trey Gowdy and Elijah Cummings requested the Government Accountability Office (GAO) to investigate actions taken by Equifax and Federal Agencies in response to the 2017 breach. The GAO report was released in August 2018.

In August 2018, I testified in three key investigations. As part of the preparation, I met with Equifax's attorneys to help prepare me for various testimonies.

Most of you reading this book will, hopefully, never have the experience of testifying in federal and state investigations. You are probably curious to understand how this process works. The investigation process does not move quickly, so there were almost twelve months from the public announcement of the breach until when I would appear to provide testimony. I also had several months' notice before I actually appeared to give evidence. This was primarily due to the need to coordinate the schedules of the attorneys and myself, as well as all the investigating staff. In some investigations, I was "invited" to provide testimony, in others, I was subpoenaed. All the investigators had some form of subpoena power so it really amounted to the same thing.

In preparing for the testimony I learned how to best respond to the investigator's questions. I discovered how important it was to carefully listen to the question being asked and answer the question specifically, without further explanation or embellishment. If the question was unclear, I asked for it to be repeated or rephrased. "I don't understand the question, could you please rephrase it?" Once I clearly understood the question, the next response was one of five standard responses: (1) yes, (2) no, (3) I don't recall, (4) I don't know, or (5) a responsive substantive answer. For example:

Q: "Mr. Payne, did you have a discussion with [someone] about the cybersecurity incident on August 1?"
A: "I don't recall" - this means that I may have had a meeting but I am not clear on the date or the specific attendees or topic.

Q: "Mr. Payne, who requested this [report]?"
A: "I don't know" - means I have no recollection or information to be able to answer that question.

I also had to ensure that I did not interrupt the investigator. The question had to be stated in its entirety before I was allowed to respond.

It was important that I was precise in responding to questions. Investigators often asked broad questions and my response needed to seek more precision. For example:

Q: "Mr. Payne, were you responsible for maintaining the Patching Policy?"
A: "Can you please clarify during what time period and also please explain what you mean by "maintaining the Patching Policy.""

Q: "During the period March 2017 to July 2017. Were you the patch policy owner?"
A: "Effective April 2017, as noted on page xx of the Patching Policy marked Exhibit 6, I was the Patch Management Policy Owner."

As a witness, I was required to tell the truth and it was perfectly acceptable to say that I did not recall or that I did not know about the question subject matter if that was the truth. This was especially challenging as the events had occurred many months or years prior to the testimony. Given this challenge in memory recall, the interviewers utilized documents that they had gained as part of their preparation to help "refresh" my memory. In all of the investigations, I was asked to review several documents such as Equifax policies, internal audit reports, email communications, internal presentations, and meeting minutes/notes. Based on the reference numbers assigned to these documents, my assumption was that hundreds of thousands (almost one million) pages of documents had been turned over to investigators by Equifax. Each document was marked as an exhibit, and a copy was handed to me and my attorney. After spending a few, or several, minutes to review the document, the investigator would ask a question about an item in the document.

For example:

Q: "Mr. Payne, do you have a copy of a document marked "Exhibit 45?"
A: "Yes."

Q: "What is this document?"
A: "It is a copy of an email that was sent to me by [someone] on April 3, 2017."

Q: "Do you recall this email?"
A: "Yes."

Q: "Can you explain what is meant by the statement [sentence from email]?" The answer would then be one of the four responses. The investigator would then ask for further explanation and if I could recall the specifics then I would provide the details as a response.

As you can see it is quite a laborious process of question → clarifying question(s) → short answer → question asking for more detail → answer with more detail. This is not a natural way in which human's normally converse and so it takes practice. In preparing for the various testimonies, I had spent several days to help practice the technique of giving testimony. When giving testimony, every spoken word in the room was captured by the stenographer. It was an intense period of focus and concentration and so I would ask for a break every 50-60 minutes just to stretch the legs and clear the mind.

By the time I actually had to appear I felt well prepared to handle the process and questioning technique.

The first appearance was in front of investigators from the Securities & Exchange Commission in Atlanta. The SEC was particularly interested in understanding what senior executives had known and when.

The following week, I was off to New York to meet with the New York State Attorney General's Office, Investor Review Board ("IRB"). This was the most grueling of all the testimonies. The IRB investigators were well prepared and really drilled down on documents and responses.

My next visit was to the U.S. House of Representatives where I met with staff from two committees, the Committee on Oversight and Government Reform and the House Energy & Commerce Committee. The room was full of between eighteen and twenty lawyers and staff, both Republicans and Democrats. Each side took an hour asking questions and then traded out to the other side for the next hour. The Committee on Oversight and Government Report (Majority Staff Report) was released in December 2018. Prior to the report's release, I was advised that they had decided to mention me by name in the report, rather than just refer to "an employee."

When the report was released, the Executive Summary stated:

"Equifax held several officials accountable for the data breach. The CIO and Chief Security Officer both took early retirements on September 15th, eight days after the public announcement. Equifax's CEO Richard Smith left the company on September 26th. On October 2nd, Equifax terminated Graeme Payne, Senior Vice President and Chief Information Officer for Global Corporate Platforms, for failing to forward an email regarding the Apache Struts vulnerability. Payne, a highly-rated employee for seven years and a senior manager of nearly 400 people, managed a number of IT systems within Equifax, including ACIS. On October 3rd, Richard Smith testified before Congress, blaming human error and a failure to communicate the need to apply a patch as underlying reasons for the breach."[68]

The Congressional report was quickly picked up by the news media and several media outlets ran articles that included my name and mentioned that I had been terminated for the breach. My testimony was quoted over

---

[68] The House Report (see page 129 footnote)

118 times in the ninety-six-page Congressional report. The report concluded: "Equifax failed to fully appreciate and mitigate its cybersecurity risks. Had the company taken action to address its observable security issues prior to this cyberattack, the data breach could have been prevented."[69]

Further in the report were some additional comments about my termination. The Committee report stated: "A senior Equifax official was terminated for failing to forward an email, an action he was not directed to do, the day before former CEO Richard Smith testified in front of Congress. This type of public relations-motivated maneuver seems gratuitous against the backdrop of all the facts."[70]

I had mixed reactions when the Congressional Report was released. On one side, I could finally talk about what happened because the report provided a tremendous amount of detail about the events leading up to the breach and the company's response. On the other, I didn't like to see my name floating around associated with the breach. Many of my friends and colleagues called when they saw the headlines posted that mentioned by name as the one terminated for causing the breach.

The House Report stated that Equifax should have addressed at least two points of failure to mitigate, or potentially prevent, the data breach:

"First, a lack of accountability and no clear lines of authority in Equifax's IT management structure existed, leading to an execution gap

---

[69] U.S. House of Representatives Committee on Oversight and Government Reform, December 2018, The Equifax Breach https://republicans-oversight.house.gov/wp-content/uploads/2018/12/Equifax-Report.pdf [hereafter referred to as "The House Report"]

[70] Ibid

between IT policy development and operation. This also restricted the company's implementation of other security initiatives in a comprehensive and timely manner. As an example, Equifax had allowed over 300 security certificates to expire, including 79 certificates for monitoring business critical domains.

Second, Equifax's aggressive growth strategy and accumulation of data resulted in a complex IT environment. Equifax ran a number of its most critical IT applications on custom-built legacy systems. Both the complexity and antiquated nature of Equifax's IT systems made IT security especially challenging. Equifax recognized the inherent security risks of operating legacy IT systems because Equifax had begun a legacy infrastructure modernization effort. This effort, however, came too late to prevent the breach."[71]

Equifax issued a several statements in response to the report. Here is one example:

"We are deeply disappointed that the committee chose not to provide us with adequate time to review and respond to a 100-page report consisting of highly technical and important information. During the few hours we were given to conduct a preliminary review, we identified significant inaccuracies and disagree with many of the factual findings," Equifax says in its statement.

"Equifax has worked in good faith for nearly 15 months with the committee to be transparent, cooperative and shed light on our learnings from the incident in order to enrich the cybersecurity community," it says. "While we believe that factual errors serve to undermine the content of the report, we are generally supportive of

---

[71] The House Report (see page 129 footnote)

many of the recommendations the committee laid out for the government and private industry to better protect consumers, and have already made significant strides in many of these areas."[72]

Class Action Lawsuits

On December 6th, 2018, the United States Judicial Panel on Multidistrict Litigation issued a Conditional Transfer Order consolidating 76 proposed class action lawsuits against Equifax to the North District of Georgia, Atlanta Division. The Panel's order went into effect on December 18th. The presiding judge is the Honorable Judge Thomas W. Thrash.

The Plaintiffs are pursuing claims against Equifax on behalf of several classes for breaching its duty to safeguard and protect the PII of the Plaintiffs and the proposed class members, injunctive relief to stop Equifax from continuing its deceptive, fraudulent and unfair business practices; restitution and/or disgorgement and compensatory damages for the economic losses and the out-of-pocket costs and damages applicable under state and federal laws.

Equifax's lawyers responded to the consolidated complaint with a motion to dismiss. As is typical in data breach cases, the Equifax lawyers argued that the plaintiffs could not prove direct financial loss or harm directly attributable to the data breach. In other words, how can a consumer know the data Equifax exposed about them is the exact data a criminal used to steal an identity or commit a crime?

---

[72] Mathew J. Schwartz, December 11, 2018, Equifax Breach 'Entirely Preventable,' House Report Finds, Bank InfoSecurity, https://www.bankinfosecurity.com/equifax-breach-entirely-preventable-house-report-finds-a-11832

On January 28th, 2019, the Court issued its Opinion and Order granting and denying in part the motion to dismiss. The Court upheld Plaintiffs' core claims being pursued–negligence and negligence per se. In addition, the Court found that Plaintiffs had pled both a duty and injury related to the theft of their personal information.

At the time of writing, Equifax had indicated that it had created a financial reserve for the settlement of the consumer class action lawsuit. The remaining class actions – financial services companies and shareholders – were still in the discovery phase.

More Congressional Hearings

Since the November 2018 elections and the change in leadership in the House of Representatives, there have been new calls to review Equifax (and other CRAs) and to develop legislation to better protect consumers. Equifax CEO Mark Begor appeared before a House Financial Services Committee on February 26th, 2019 along with the CEOs of the other two credit reporting agencies for a hearing entitled: *"Who's Keeping Score? Holding Credit Bureaus Accountable and Repairing a Broken System."*

"House Financial Services Committee Chairwoman Maxine Waters blasted Equifax and its competitors at a Washington hearing, claiming the companies have actually tried to take advantage of the 2017 hack to sell new data-security services to customers. Representative Patrick McHenry, the panel's top Republican, argued that because Equifax, TransUnion and Experian Plc dominate the industry, they have little incentive to put consumers' interests first....The Equifax hack compromised the information of more than 140 million people, making it one of the most sweeping data breaches ever. While the incident

triggered days of congressional hearings, industry critics have said it resulted in few reforms. Waters, who took over the financial services committee in January, has promised to change that by tightening regulation of credit-reporting companies...She also introduced legislation this week that would strengthen consumer protections and shorten the amount of time negative financial information can remain on reports. "We need to ask whether the system is so beyond repair that we need to completely rebuild the entire consumer-credit reporting sector to truly put consumers first," California's Waters said at the hearing...[73]

In November 2018, Marriott announced an even larger breach than the 2017 Equifax Breach. Hackers gained access to the reservation systems of many of Marriott's hotel chains for the prior four years. The breach exposed private details of up to 500 million customers, including names, addresses, credit card numbers, phone numbers, passport numbers, travel locations and arrival and departure dates.

On March 7th, 2019, the Senate Permanent Subcommittee on Investigations held a hearing "Examining Private Sector Data Breaches." Equifax CEO Mark Begor and Marriott CEO Arne Sorensen appeared before the Committee. Earlier that day, the Subcommittee released a report on the Equifax Data Breach. Most of the findings in this report had already been covered by the December 2018 House of Representatives' report and the GAO August 2018 report. I was not asked to testify for the Senate Report.

---

[73] Austin Weinstein, February 26th, 2019, Equifax Faces Fresh D.C. Fury With Democrats in Control of House, Bloomberg, https://www.bloomberg.com/news/articles/2019-02-26/equifax-faces-fresh-d-c-fury-with-democrats-in-control-of-house

The Report main findings were:

- Equifax failed to prioritize cybersecurity;
- Equifax could not follow its own policies in patching the vulnerability that ultimately caused the breach.
- Equifax failed to locate and patch Apache Struts;
- Equifax left itself open to attack due to poor cybersecurity practices;
- The damage done by the hackers could have been minimized;
- Equifax waited six weeks before notifying the public it was breached;
- Equifax executives believed they did all they could to prevent the breach;
- TransUnion and Experian avoided a breach;
- Equifax failed to preserve key internal chat records.

The report concluded: "Equifax response to the March 2017 cybersecurity vulnerability that facilitated the breach was inadequate and hampered by Equifax's neglect of cybersecurity. Equifax's shortcomings are long-standing and reflect a broader culture of complacency toward cybersecurity preparedness. The Subcommittee also lacks full understanding of the breach, as a company failed to preserve relevant messages sent over an internal messaging platform."[74]

---

[74] United States Senate Committee on Homeland Security and Government Affairs, Permanent Subcommittee on Investigations, February 2019, How Equifax Neglected Cybersecurity and Suffered a Devastating Data Breach, https://www.hsgac.senate.gov/imo/media/doc/FINAL%20Equifax%20Report.pdf

Increasing Costs

The 2017 data breach and its aftermath have incurred a high cost to Equifax. As reported in their SEC filings, the company has spent $565 million ($440 million net of insurance proceeds) through the end of 2018 and is planning on spending another $350 million in 2019. By the end of 2019, Equifax will have spent $200 million in legal costs and $82 million product liability costs. The product liability costs are the cost of providing TrustedID® Premier, the credit file monitoring and identity theft protection product, that was provided for free to all eligible U.S. consumers who signed up through January 31st, 2018. Equifax decided to offer a further twelve months of free credit monitoring and identity protection services for consumers, but rather than offer their own TrustedID Premier product, they are providing Experian® IDNotify™ at no cost to the consumer.

Equifax Costs to Date ($m):

	2017	2018	2019 Estimate
Legal and Investigative Fees	$75.5	$73.6	$50.0
Technology and Data Security	$26.5	$307.2	$300.0
Product Liability	$62.0	$20	$-
Gross Expenses	**$164.0**	**$401.2**	**$350.0**
Insurance Recoveries	*($50.0)*	*($75.0)*	*$-*
Net Expenses	**$114.0**	**$326.2**	**$350.0**

Not included in the above table are estimates of fines and litigation settlements that will inevitably arise as a result of the multiple legal actions and investigations currently underway. In some cases, regulatory bodies have notified their intent to fine Equifax but have not determined the amount. The company stated in their 2018 10-K:

"While we believe it is reasonably possible that we will incur losses associated with such proceedings and investigations, it is not possible at this time to estimate the amount of loss or range of possible loss that might result from adverse judgments, settlements, penalties or other resolution of the proceedings and investigations...The Company believes that the ultimate amount paid on these actions, claims and investigations could be material to the Company's consolidated financial condition, results of operations, or cash flows in future periods."

How much could Equifax end up paying in fines and settlements is anyone's guess. The Federal Trade Commission has yet to fine Yahoo for its data breach.

In addition, Equifax has been undertaking "substantial initiatives in security and consumer support, and a company-wide transformation of our technology infrastructure, which we refer to as our technology transformation." By the end of 2020, the company will have spent close to $1.2 billion on this technology transformation. While not disclosed, I would expect Equifax is also paying higher costs for insurance, finance/audit and compliance activities in 2019.

Equifax also made substantial disclosures in its 2017 and 2018 SEC filings regarding the "2017 Cybersecurity Incident."

2017 Cybersecurity Incident

In 2017, we experienced a cybersecurity incident following a criminal attack on our systems that involved the theft of certain personally identifiable information of U.S., Canadian and U.K. consumers. Criminals exploited a software vulnerability in a U.S. website application to gain unauthorized access to our network. In March 2017, the U.S. Department of Homeland Security distributed a notice concerning the software vulnerability. We undertook efforts to identify and remediate vulnerable systems; however, the vulnerability in the website application that was exploited was not identified by our security processes. We discovered unusual network activity in late-July 2017 and upon discovery, promptly investigated the activity. Once the activity was identified as potential unauthorized access, we acted to stop the intrusion and engaged a leading, independent cybersecurity firm to conduct a forensic investigation to determine the scope of the unauthorized access, including the specific information impacted. Based on our forensic investigation, the unauthorized access occurred from mid-May 2017 through July 2017. No evidence was found that the Company's core consumer, employment and income, or commercial reporting databases were accessed. We continue to cooperate with law enforcement in connection with the criminal investigation into the actors responsible for the 2017 cybersecurity incident.

The Company has taken actions to provide consumers with tools to protect credit data. Immediately following the announcement of the 2017 cybersecurity incident, the Company devoted substantial resources to notify people of the incident and to provide free services to assist people in monitoring their credit and identity information.

This included making its TrustedID® Premier service, an identity theft protection and credit file monitoring product, available for free to all U.S. consumers for twelve months for those who signed up by January 31, 2018. In late 2018, the Company extended the free credit file monitoring services for impacted consumers in the U.S. using the free TrustedID Premier® service by providing them the opportunity to enroll in Experian® IDNotify™ at no cost for an additional twelve months. Similarly, for impacted consumers in Canada and the U.K., we provided free credit reports and scores, credit monitoring and identity theft protection for twenty four months. As part of our commitment to providing long-term resources and protections for consumers, in January 2018, the Company introduced Lock & Alert™, a mobile application enabled service that allows U.S. consumers to quickly lock and unlock their Equifax credit report for free, for life.

As a result of the 2017 cybersecurity incident, we are party to numerous lawsuits and governmental investigations. See "Item 1A. Risk Factors" and "Item 3. Legal Proceedings" in this Form 10-K for more information regarding these lawsuits and investigations.

Legal Troubles

When a company has a large public data breach, you can guarantee there will be class action lawsuits and regulatory investigations. The large scale of the 2017 Equifax Data Breach has led to hundreds of legal actions against the company. State and Federal regulators in the U.S.,

Canada and the United Kingdom have launched investigations. Let's take a look at the more significant legal troubles Equifax is now facing.

Multidistrict Litigation

Equifax received hundreds of class actions and other lawsuits as a result of the 2017 Data Breach. The plaintiffs in these cases are classes representing U.S. consumers, small businesses, and financial institutions. The class action suits are seeking monetary damages and other relief. Financial institutions are claiming their businesses have been placed at risk as a result of the Equifax Data Breach.

The City of Chicago alleged Equifax violated state laws and local ordinances governing protection of personal data, consumer fraud, breach notice requirements and business practices. Three Indian Tribes filed suits in federal court on behalf of themselves and other similarly situated federally recognized Indian Tribes and Nations. The Commonwealth of Puerto Rico filed an action on its own behalf and on behalf of the people of Puerto Rico. All of these cases were consolidated into a single multi-district case in December 2017. The case was moved to be under the jurisdiction of the Northern District of Georgia.

Equifax attempted to dismiss the consolidated class action complaints. On January 28th, 2019, the Court dismissed the small businesses' consolidated class action complaint in its entirety and allowed most of the claims brought by the consumer and financial institution plaintiffs. The case is proceeding through discovery and pre-trial motions as I write this in April 2019.

Other Litigation

A consolidated class action lawsuit has been filed against Equifax and several past and present executives alleging violations of various federal securities laws in connection with statements and alleged omissions regarding Equifax's cybersecurity systems and controls. This group claims that shareholders who purchased shares between February 25th, 2016 and September 15th, 2017 were harmed.

A consolidated shareholder derivative action naming certain current and former executives, officers and directors, and Equifax itself, as defendants has been filed in federal court. The consolidated complaint alleges claims for breaches of fiduciary duties, unjust enrichment, corporate waste and insider selling by certain defendants, as well as certain claims under the federal securities laws.

The City of San Francisco filed a lawsuit against Equifax in Superior Court in the City of San Francisco on behalf of the People of the State of California alleging violations of California's unfair competition law due to purported violations of statutory protections of personal data and statutory data breach requirements, and seeking statutory penalties and restitution for Californian consumers.

Civil enforcement actions have been filed against Equifax by the Attorneys General of Massachusetts and West Virginia alleging violations of commonwealth/state consumer protection laws. The Puerto Rico Department of Consumer Affairs has issued Notices of Infraction related to Equifax's alleged failure to give timely notice of the data breach under Puerto Rico law to the Department and Puerto Rico consumers.

Over 1,000 individual consumer actions, including multi-plaintiff actions, have been filed against Equifax in state (general jurisdiction and small claims) and federal courts. These claims include more than 2,500 individual plaintiffs. In addition, there are approximately fifty individual arbitration claims.

These various suits and claims will continue to work through the courts and legal system over the next 12-18 months. Many may result in settlement prior to reaching trial.

Investigations

In addition, numerous governmental agencies are investigating Equifax. These investigations may result in fines, settlements or other relief against the company. Investigations in progress include:

- 48 state Attorneys General offices
- Separate investigations from State Attorney General offices of Massachusetts, West Virginia, Puerto Rico, Indiana and Texas
- District of Columbia
- New York State Attorney General Investor Protection Bureau ("IPB")
- New York Department of Financial Services
- Federal Trade Commission
- Consumer Financial Protection Bureau
- U.S. Securities and Exchange Commission ("SEC")
- U.S. Department of Justice,
- Office of the Privacy Commissioner of Canada
- U.K.'s Financial Conduct Authority

Based on what has happened in other large breaches, I would suspect Equifax will receive fines and agree to some form of sustained close monitoring, including independent audits of its cybersecurity controls.

Business Results Suffer

In the immediate aftermath of the 2017 Data Breach, some Equifax larger customers switched services to other Equifax competitors. It is also likely Equifax did not have the same sales opportunities for new business in the months following the breach. Most of this impact can be seen in 2018.

In 2018, the revenue growth that had been averaging in double digits over the last few years fell to 1%. The burden of remediation and legal costs is also impacting the operating margins.

Equifax Operating Performance - Fiscal Years 2016-2018[75]

	Key Performance Indicators Twelve Months Ended December 31,		
	2018	**2017**	**2016**
	(In millions, except per share data)		
Operating revenue	$ 3,412.1	$ 3,362.2	$ 3,144.9
Operating revenue change	1%	7%	18%
Operating income	$ 448.0	$ 831.7	$ 825.1
Operating margin	13.1 %	24.7 %	26.2 %
Net income attributable to Equifax	$ 299.8	$ 587.3	$ 488.8
Diluted earnings per share	$ 2.47	$ 4.83	$ 4.04
Cash provided by operating activities	$ 672.2	$ 816.0	$ 823.0
Capital expenditures*	$ (368.1)	$ (214.0)	$ (191.5)

*Amounts above include accruals for capital expenditures.

Equifax stated in its most recent annual report: "The Company believes the ultimate amount paid on these actions, claims and investigations could be material to the Company's consolidated financial condition, results of operations, or cash flows in future periods and may reduce available resources to invest in technology and innovation."

---

[75] Equifax 2019 10-K filed with the Securities and Exchange Commission

There does not appear to be a consensus on how long the Equifax financial results will be burdened by the costs of remediation and ongoing legal actions. As of writing, the stock price has recovered to around $125 per share. Several large institutional investors purchased shares over the last eighteen months in anticipation of a return to future earnings levels and growth.

Equifax New Security First Culture

Since the 2017 Data Breach, Equifax has made some significant changes to improve the culture of cybersecurity in the company. In February 2018, the company hired Jamil Farshchi as the Chief Information Security Officer, reporting directly to the CEO.

Farshchi had previously been the CISO at The Home Depot where he managed the aftermath of their data breach and implemented a post-breach remediation plan. Having the CISO as part of the Equifax Senior Leadership Team is a good move and will help to keep the right focus on security at the top of the company.

Equifax has publicly reported on the three-year initiative that is underway to transform its security processes, technology and infrastructure. Equifax has significantly bolstered the size of the information security team to help create a "security-first" culture. They claim to have increased the number of technical resources so that 75% of the security organization is technical vs. non-technical.

The company is attempting to take a leadership role in promoting cybersecurity in the business community and among its customers and peers. They have created an organization to help CISOs in Atlanta and have been promoting cybersecurity at various events and forums around the world.

Equifax has also "refined its security policies and technical standards and regained compliance certifications."

They are working on improving the cybersecurity capabilities, including: enhanced risk-based decision-making, improving data insights, integrating with the cloud transformation and expanding the breadth and depth of detection, response, and recovery capabilities.

The Equifax Board of Directors announced an enhanced Board oversight plan in its 2018 Annual Proxy Statement. The plan included:

1. Heightened Board-level Engagement. The Board reported it had met seventy-five times since the breach and had enhanced its attention to cybersecurity risks and trends, and the Company's approach to managing those risks.
2. Broadened Technology Committee Responsibilities. The Board tasked the Technology Committee with specific oversight of cybersecurity and technology risks and management's efforts to monitor and mitigate those risks. They also expect that the Technology Committee will engage independent experts to help it fulfil its responsibilities.
3. Formed Special Committee. This special committee reviewed the 2017 data breach and the company's response.
4. Enhanced Cybersecurity Defenses. Investments to enhance technical controls and procedures. Hiring a new CISO and adding personnel to the security team.

5. Enhanced Risk Escalation and Disclosure Controls. Enabling rapid escalation and internal notification to senior management and the Board.

6. Implemented Changes to ERM Program. Adopting the "three lines of defense" model for establishing effective checks and balances.

I am pleased Equifax is making these changes. Changing the culture of an organization takes a long time and setting the right tone from the top is a critical part of the change process.

* * * *

The bottom line is that Equifax was not ignoring cybersecurity—far from it. There was a lot of focus and spend on closing cybersecurity gaps.

As Susan Mauldin stated in testimony to the U.S. House of Representatives:

"I think we had a lot of good work...But I think it just simply - for me, it underscores the importance of staying aware and staying vigilant, staying ahead of the threat actor. They are so sophisticated and so well-funded that every company has to be continuously on its toes and pushing ahead...vigorously to get things done, get plans completed, and so forth."[76]

---

[76] The House Report (see page 129 footnote)

Recovering from a major data breach is not a simple task. It can take several years (maybe decades) for a company to rebuild trust with consumers, regulators, customers, and industry observers.

This all costs money, and while the company is investing in big initiatives like developing a security-first culture and migrating systems to the cloud, savings must be made in other areas to offset these costs. Since I left Equifax, there have been several reorganizations and employee reductions. Many good friends and former colleagues have lost their jobs. In the fourth quarter of 2018, the company recognized a $46 million charge for workforce reduction costs. I have no doubt Equifax will be stronger in the long run.

The 2017 Equifax Data Breach and its aftermath raise some broader questions about some important issues. Do we have the right framework in place in the U.S. to protect consumers' personal information? What should be done to reduce the reliance on Social Security Numbers? What role should Boards of Directors play in overseeing cybersecurity preparedness? What remedies should be available to consumers when companies fail to protect their personal information? How should we defend ourselves from nation-state cyberattacks? These topics are explored in Chapter 8.

Part III – Broader Lessons and Recommendations

Chapter Eight –
A New Path Forward

In this chapter, I will discuss some of the broader lessons we can learn from the 2017 Equifax Data Breach and other large data breaches that have occurred in the last few years. One thing is for sure, data breaches will continue and consumers' personal information will continue to be exposed. Companies will continue to work to protect sensitive data.

In our highly digitized world, data is a valuable resource that will continue to be sought-after by cybercriminals for financial gain or to advance a cause, and by nation states for espionage and furtherance of their strategic goals.

Protecting Consumer Personal Information

Do we have the right framework in place in the U.S. to protect consumer personal information?

Many U.S. consumers were surprised to find that Equifax had extensive data about them. In the U.S., we have not approached data privacy from a top-down model. In many other countries, especially in Europe, data privacy is considered a fundamental human right. The OECD came out with a set of Privacy Principles in 1980.

OECD Privacy Principles[77]

1. Collection Limitation Principle - There should be limits to the collection of personal data and any such data should be obtained by lawful and fair means and, where appropriate, with the knowledge or consent of the data subject.

2. Data Quality Principle - Personal data should be relevant to the purposes for which they are to be used, and, to the extent necessary for those purposes, should be accurate, complete and kept up-to-date.

3. Purpose Specification Principle - The purposes for which personal data are collected should be specified not later than at the time of data collection and the subsequent use limited to the fulfilment of those purposes or such others as are not incompatible with those purposes and as are specified on each occasion of change of purpose.

4. Use Limitation Principle - Personal data should not be disclosed, made available or otherwise used for purposes other than those specified in accordance with Paragraph 9 except: a) with the consent of the data subject; or b) by the authority of law.

5. Security Safeguards Principle - Personal data should be protected by reasonable security safeguards against such risks as loss or unauthorized access, destruction, use, modification or disclosure of data.

6. Openness Principle - There should be a general policy of openness

---

[77] http://oecdprivacy.org/

about developments, practices and policies with respect to personal data. Means should be readily available of establishing the existence and nature of personal data, and the main purposes of their use, as well as the identity and usual residence of the data controller.

7. Individual Participation Principle - An individual should have the right:

a) to obtain from a data controller, or otherwise, confirmation of whether or not the data controller has data relating to him;

b) to have communicated to him, data relating to him:
    i) within a reasonable time;
    ii) at a charge, if any, that is not excessive;
    iii) in a reasonable manner; and
    iv) in a form that is readily intelligible to him;

c) to be given reasons if a request made under subparagraphs (a) and (b) is denied, and to be able to challenge such denial; and

d) to challenge data relating to him and, if the challenge is successful to have the data erased, rectified, completed or amended.

8. Accountability Principle - A data controller should be accountable for complying with measures which give effect to the principles stated above.

After the OECD Data Principles were published, many countries adopted national privacy rules and legislation. Before I came to the U.S., I lived in New Zealand. Back in the 1990s, we had a national Privacy Act and a Privacy Ombudsman who helped implement the rules that generally followed the OECD Principles. The European Union adopted the Data Protection Directive (officially Directive 95/46/EC on the protection of individuals with regard to the processing of personal data and on the free movement of such data) in 1995.

More recently, the EU has adopted expanded rules known as the GDPR (General Data Privacy Rules - EU) 2016/679). GDPR essentially provides for the data protection and privacy of all individuals within the EU, giving control to individuals over their personal data. The GDPR rules require controllers of personal data to implement "appropriate technical and organizational measures" to meet the data protection principles. Business processes that handle personal data must be designed and built with consideration of the principles and provide safeguards to protect data, and use the highest possible privacy settings by default, so that the data is not available publicly without explicit, informed consent, and cannot be used to identify a subject without additional information stored separately.

Under GDPR, no personal data may be processed unless it is done under a lawful basis specified by the regulation, or unless the data controller or processor has received an unambiguous and individualized affirmation of consent from the data subject. The data subject has the right to revoke this consent at any time.

A processor of personal data must clearly disclose any data collection, declare the lawful basis and purpose for data processing, and state how long data is being retained and if it is being shared with any third parties. Data subjects (consumers) have the right to request a portable copy of the data collected by a processor in a common format and to have their data erased under certain circumstances. Businesses must report any data breaches within seventy-two hours if the breach would have an adverse effect on user privacy. GDPR violators may be fined up to €20 million or up to 4% of the annual worldwide turnover.

In the U.S., we have taken piecemeal approaches through federal legislation. The Fair Credit Reporting Act 1970 requires credit reporting agencies to have processes for consumers to notify CRAs of errors in their credit reports and for data furnishers to investigate these disputes within a specified time.

Financial services firms that provide financial products are subject to certain privacy and security requirements contained in Gramm-Leach-Bliley Act. Healthcare privacy is covered under the Healthcare Insurance Portability and Accountability Act (HIPAA). Much of the focus of these requirements is on consumer notice and consent. We have all received the numerous pages of privacy disclosures when opening a bank account or checking in at a healthcare provider. The Children's Online Privacy Act ("COPA") deals with the protection of children's privacy rights online and requires parental permission to gather data about children under the age of thirteen years.

In the absence of strong overarching federal rules, State governments have moved to protect consumer privacy rights. Every U.S. state now has privacy legislation of some type. While the coverage of what is defined as personal information and the requirements to protect it vary widely, all states now have some form of breach notification rule.

States started enacting breach notification laws after the widely-publicized 2005 ChoicePoint data breach (see Chapter 1). Californian consumers were the only ones notified of this breach because California was the only state at the time with a mandatory breach notification law. Since then, all fifty states plus the District of Columbia, Puerto Rico,

Guam, and the Virgin Islands have implemented rules requiring notification to individuals when their personal information[78] has been compromised.

Recently, California has enacted the California Privacy Protection Act (CPPA) modeled after the European GDPR. CPPA gives consumers in California four basic rights in relation to their personal information:

1. the right to know what personal information a business has collected about them, where it was sourced from, what it is being used for, whether it is being disclosed or sold, and to whom it is being disclosed or sold;
2. the right to opt out of allowing a business to sell their personal information to third parties;
3. the right to have a business delete their personal information, with some exceptions; and
4. the right to receive equal service and pricing from a business, even if they exercise their privacy rights under the Act.

There have been several attempts by Congress to enact broader federal laws over the years. All have failed. One challenge is, who would administer a federal privacy law? Today, the Federal Trade Commission has broad responsibility under the unfair trade practices rules to investigate and levy administrative orders and fines on companies that do not follow their stated privacy policies. However, other federal agencies have some specific authority over certain entities.

For example, the Department of Health and Human Services is responsible for enforcing privacy rules under HIPAA (Healthcare

---

[78] The definition of personal information varies between states

Insurance Portability and Accountability Act). The challenge for U.S. corporations is that they must be aware of and comply with a myriad of privacy legislation across all the states in which they operate. I do see value in establishing overarching privacy rules at the federal level but I am not confident this will occur in the near future. We are likely to continue to have states setting ever-increasing requirements to protect their consumers.

I also believe there should be greater transparency about how credit reporting agencies collect and use data about consumers. In the U.S. House Committee on Oversight & Government Reform investigation, the committee recommended credit reporting agencies "offer consumers a free, simple summary explaining the data collected on the individual…[and] the number of times the CRA provided their data to a business in the last year. The summary should be available to the consumer to view at any time, outside the free annual credit report offer."[79]

As part of the fallout of the Equifax breach, Congress passed legislation requiring credit reporting agencies to offer free credit freezes to consumers.[80]

In addition, Equifax developed a new product that offers, for free, the ability for a consumer to lock their credit report. The Equifax lock product uses a mobile application allowing a user to lock and unlock their report. The lock product is only applied to your Equifax credit report. Equifax has publicly stated that they will provide this product free forever.

---

[79] The House Report (see page 129 footnote)
[80] The Economic Growth, Regulatory Relief and Consumer Protection Act 2018.

A "lock" and a credit freeze have the same impact on your Equifax credit report, but aren't the same thing.

Both generally prevent access to your Equifax credit report; unless you temporarily lift or permanently remove a freeze, or unlock your Equifax credit report, it can't be accessed to open new accounts.[81] Credit freezes are federally regulated and a PIN is required to temporarily lift or permanently remove a freeze.

Since September 2018, placing, lifting and removing a credit freeze is free at each of the credit reporting agencies, giving consumers more control over how their credit report is used; this is a move in the right direction and I hope the other credit reporting agencies take similar steps.

---

[81] There are a few exceptions: companies providing credit monitoring services; companies providing you with a copy of your report when requested by you; federal, state, and local governments and courts in certain circumstances; companies using the information in connection with the underwriting of insurance, or for employment, tenant or background screening purposes; companies that have a current account or relationship with you, and collection agencies acting on behalf of those whom you owe; companies that authenticate a consumer's identity for purposes other than granting credit, or for investigating or preventing actual or potential fraud; and companies that wish to make pre-approved offers of credit or insurance to you.

Over-Reliance on Social Security Numbers

What should be done to reduce the reliance on Social Security Numbers?

The Social Security Number ("SSN") was created with one purpose in mind: "to uniquely identify U.S. workers, enabling employers to submit accurate reports of covered earnings for use in administering benefits under the new Social Security program."[82]

The Social Security Act 1935 required that employers begin deducting payroll taxes from a worker's wages. The Social Security Board needed to establish a way to easily track the earnings of tens of millions of individuals. The Board did not want to use employee names and addresses because these were not unique enough. Some consideration was given to using fingerprints, but this was not pursued due to concerns that this technique was associated with the identification of criminals.

A numbering scheme was created to identify employees (SSNs) and employers (EINs). After much debate and study, the Board arrived at a numbering scheme that had a nine-digit number consisting of a three-digit area code, a two-digit group number, and a four-digit serial number.

SSNs and social security cards were never intended to serve as proof of identification.

---

[82] Carolyn Puckett, Social Security Bulletin, Vol. 69, No. 2, 2009, The Story of the Social Security Number, Social Security Administration website, https://www.ssa.gov/policy/docs/ssb/v69n2/v69n2p55.html

"The card was never intended to serve as a personal identification document—that is, it does not establish that the person presenting the card is actually the person whose name and SSN appear on the card. Although SSA has made the card counterfeit-resistant, the card does not contain information that would allow it to be used as proof of identity."[83]

The problem was, there was a certain simplicity and efficiency of using the SSN since most people had one. Before long, other government departments and private enterprises were using the SSN to help in their recordkeeping. Federal law did not preclude the use of the SSN by private enterprises. The number sequence was easily processed in early computer systems that kept records of individuals. In fact, an Executive Order in 1943 required federal agencies to use the SSN for the purpose of identifying individuals in any new record systems.

As more and more government and private enterprise records became computerized, concerns arose about how the SSN was being used as a kind of national identifier. In 1971, the Social Security Administration studied the use of the SSN and proposed a "cautious and conservative" position and to do nothing to promote its use as an identifier. Nevertheless, Congressional legislation and federal agency regulations continued to require the collection of SSNs for myriad purposes.

The universal nature of SSNs has helped facilitate increasing identify theft. SSNs were printed on many forms of government-issued identity cards for several decades until this was prohibited. Employer records, healthcare records, banking records, criminal databases, and credit

---

[83] Ibid

reports all have used SSNs to help identify individuals. The SSNs are frequently printed on reports produced from these systems.

Furthermore, many employers, financial institutions, health insurers and providers, use social security numbers to help identify individuals in online systems when creating accounts, registering for services and to validate identities in a "forgot password" process.

The FTC estimates that as many as nine million Americans have their identities stolen each year. The Equifax 2017 Data Breach exposed SSNs of half of the U.S. population.

SSNs are the "key to the kingdom" for identity thieves. Criminals with access to a consumer's SSN could potentially file tax returns, open accounts, take out lines of credit and commit many other forms of fraud. SSNs can be purchased on the dark web for less than $1. Consumers cannot protect themselves from misuse of their SSN. The Social Security Administration has very limited ability to reissue SSNs.

With increasing data breaches in the 2000's, there have been many calls for the government to rethink the use of SSNs. There is a need to break the link between the use of the SSN as an identifier and as an authenticator. Identifiers can be public, for example our social media handles. Authenticators require secrecy, helping to validate we are the right person by using something we know (a secret like a password), something we have (like a physical access card), or something we are (like a biometric fingerprint or iris scan).

SSNs are not secret anymore and should not be used as authenticators. The U.S. House investigation into the 2017 Equifax Data Breach also emphasized this point:

"Social Security numbers are widely used in the public and private sector to both identify and authenticate individuals...Attackers stole the Social Security numbers of 145 million consumers from Equifax. As a result of this breach, nearly half of the country's Social Security numbers are no longer confidential. To better protect consumers from identity theft...relevant federal agencies should pursue emerging technology solutions as an alternative to Social Security Number use."[84]

Improving Corporate Governance of Cybersecurity

What role should Boards of Directors play in overseeing cybersecurity preparedness?

There is no doubt that the nature of business has changed over the last twenty to thirty years. The advent of computerized systems in business in the 1960's and the rapid growth in technology innovation has completely changed the business landscape. Just look at the Fortune 500; only sixty companies in that list in 1995 remain in the F500 today. Every company has moved into a far more digitized environment where company value is derived from data and intellectual property as opposed to physical infrastructure and goods alone.

There has also been a corresponding growth in cyber risk, including cybersecurity. A recent World Economic Forum study[85] identified cybersecurity as the number two risk. The National Association of Corporate Directors in 2017 published a paper entitled "NACD

---

[84] The House Report (see page 129 footnote)
[85] World Economic Forum, January 15th, 2019, The Global Risks Report 2019, https://www.weforum.org/reports/the-global-risks-report-2019

Director's Handbook on Cyber-Risk Oversight." The paper identifies five principles the corporate directors should follow in helping to manage cybersecurity in their organizations.

"Leading Companies view cyber-risk in the same way they do other critical risks - in terms of a risk-reward trade-off... As the complexity of...attacks increases, so does the risk they pose to the corporations.... Cyberattacks can have a severe impact on the organization's reputation and brand... At the same time, the motivation to deploy new and emerging technologies in order to lower costs, improve customer service, and drive innovation, is stronger than ever. These competing pressures on corporate staff and business leaders mean that conscientious and comprehensive oversight at the Board level is essential..."[86]

---

[86] National Association of Corporate Directors, January 12th, 2017, NACD Director's Handbook on Cyber-Risk Oversight,
https://www.nacdonline.org/insights/publications.cfm?ItemNumber=10687
[hereafter referred to as "NACD Director's Handbook on Cyber-Risk Oversight"]

National Association of Corporate Directors Cyber-Risk Principles[87]

Principle 1: Directors need to understand and approach cybersecurity is an enterprise-wide risk management issue, not just an IT issue

Principle 2: Directors should understand the legal implications of cyber-risks as they relate to their company's specific circumstances

Principle 3: Boards should have adequate access to cybersecurity expertise, and discussions about cyber-risk management should be given regular and adequate time on Board Meeting agendas

Principle 4: Directors should set the expectation that management will establish an enterprise-wide cyber-risk management framework with adequate staffing and budget

Principle 5: Board-management discussions about cyber-risk should include identification of which risks to avoid, which to accept, and which to mitigate or transfer through insurance, as well as specific plans associated with each approach.

A similar set of guidelines has been issued by the Directors and Chief Risk Officers Group (DCRO) - "Guiding Principles for Cyber Risk Governance: Principles for Directors in Overseeing Cybersecurity."[88] Both the NACD and DCRO guidelines are sound and should be read and followed by all corporate Boards. One of the challenges of these

---

[87] Ibid

[88] DCRO, June 2018, GUIDING PRINCIPLES FOR CYBER RISK GOVERNANCE: Principles for Directors in Overseeing Cybersecurity, https://dcro.org/

principles is that the Board needs to be educated and have the right expertise to help evaluate the strategies and actions be taken by management. This, to me, is one of the major challenges facing Boards today and one of the reasons I am focused on helping Boards and senior executives in cybersecurity.

One frequent question I get is, how much should we be spending on cybersecurity? It is a good question but not an easy one to answer. There are certainly benchmarks that report security spend as a certain percentage of revenue or IT spend, but these can be deceiving. Spending money in and of itself does not necessarily mean the company is more secure or better prepared to respond to a security incident. So many factors go into that equation, and rather than focusing on spend, I encourage Boards to focus on understanding the risks and tradeoffs against those risks.

It is interesting to see that Equifax's Board is now more fully engaged in deliberations over cybersecurity. The Equifax Board of Directors announced an enhanced Board oversight plan in its 2018 Annual Proxy Statement.

The plan included tasking the "Technology Committee with specific oversight of cybersecurity and technology risks and management's efforts to monitor and mitigate those risks."[89] They also expected that the Technology Committee would engage independent experts to help it fulfil its responsibilities. The Board also "enhanced risk escalation and disclosure controls. Enabling rapid escalation and internal notification to senior management and the Board."

---

[89] Equifax 2018 Proxy Statement filed with the Securities and Exchange Commission

These steps are a positive move toward achieving the five principles identified by the NACD. Equifax also modified the annual performance incentive program for executives to align with the security objectives.

With increasing cybersecurity breaches occurring, it is also likely the Securities and Exchange Commission will want to see enhanced disclosures by public companies regarding cyber-risks and incidents. At the time of writing, the most recent guidance from the SEC had been issued in February 2018:

"Cybersecurity risks pose grave threats to investors, our capital markets, and our country. Whether it is the companies in which investors invest, their accounts with financial services firms, the markets through which they trade, or the infrastructure they count on daily, the investing public and the US economy depends on the security and reliability of information and communications technology, systems, and networks." [90]

The 2018 guidance added to earlier guidance issued by the SEC in 2011. The earlier guidance clarified companies' obligations to disclose cybersecurity risks, material breaches and the potential impact of the breaches on business, finances and operations.

The 2018 guidance added two new topics: (i) the importance of public companies having strong disclosure controls and procedures to enable

---

[90] SECURITIES AND EXCHANGE COMMISSION, 17 CFR Parts 229 and 249, [Release Nos. 33-10459; 34-82746], February 21st, 2018, Commission Statement and Guidance on Public Company Cybersecurity Disclosures, https://www.sec.gov/news/press-release/2018-22

timely and accurate disclosure of cybersecurity risks and incidents, and (ii) insider trading prohibitions as related to cybersecurity incidents.

In September 2018, EY released a report[91] that studied disclosures by public companies. The study concluded: "Most companies disclosed that cybersecurity is among the risks overseen by the Board and whether any committees are charged with oversight responsibilities regarding cybersecurity. How management reports to the Board on this topic is an emerging area for disclosure with less than half of companies disclosing this information and a smaller subset offering detail around the frequency of that reporting and what it includes."[92]

On the topic of director qualification, the report concluded:

"Forty-one percent of companies include cybersecurity experience as among the key director qualifications highlighted or considered by the Board. The disclosure does not always indicate which directors (if any) have this expertise, and there are variations in what is considered cybersecurity expertise."[93]

Over time, I am hopeful that Boards continue to recruit or bring in appropriate cybersecurity expertise to help them understand cybersecurity risks and evaluate the effectiveness of the organizations' cybersecurity preparedness.

---

[91] EY, 2018, Cybersecurity disclosure benchmarking, ey.com
https://www.ey.com/us/en/issues/governance-and-reporting/ey-cybersecurity-disclosure-benchmarking
[92] Ibid
[93] Ibid

Consumer Remedies After a Breach

What remedies should be made available to consumers who suffer from data breaches?

I discussed in Chapter 1 the number of large data breaches that have occurred in the 21st Century. According to a study by Risk Based Security, the number of publicly-reported data breaches in 2018 was 6,500, resulting in the disclosure of 5 billion records.[94] This was actually down from the 2017 figures.

The reality is that data breaches will continue. When consumer data is exposed, a standard response by companies is to provide one year's free credit report monitoring and identity protection. All the "big three" credit reporting agencies provide these services. While the products differ between the three bureaus, they typically include:

- 3-Bureau credit monitoring
- Identity theft monitoring
- Credit report alerts
- Dark web surveillance
- Lock and unlock of credit report
- Identity theft insurance.

The credit reporting agencies charge around $20 per month for this service so the retail value of a year's monitoring is $240. When these

---

[94] Risk Based Security, 2019, 2018 Data Breach Trends, https://pages.riskbasedsecurity.com/2018-ye-breach-quickview-report

products are sold in bulk, they are considerably discounted to the company that has suffered the breach.

The problem with many large data breaches is that the data exposed may not be used for a long time. The exposed data may sit idle and not be used by criminals or nation states for years, maybe even decades. In addition, credit monitoring really focuses on the opening and closing of new accounts and changes in balances. It may not detect a payment fraud or someone using your identity to obtain a passport or a tax return. Some people don't understand what they are actually receiving with credit monitoring and may be assuming a "false sense of security."

The U.S. House Committee on Oversight and Government Reform recommended that the GAO review the effectiveness of identity monitoring and protection services offered to breach victims. Others have called for these services to be provided for longer periods. In the Equifax case, the company decided to extend credit monitoring and identity protection for another year through to the end of 2019, this time using Experian rather than its own product.

In the absence of prolonged credit monitoring and identity protection services, we consumers need to recognize that our data has probably been exposed and act on that basis:

"...you should live your life assuming that your information is already compromised and act accordingly. What does this mean? It means you should be routinely checking your credit reports, analyzing your bank and credit card statements, keeping an eye on mail received at your

home (as well as your email inbox) and practicing smart cybersecurity habits on all of your devices—including your phone. "[95]

The Privacy Rights Clearinghouse provides some good advice on what to do when certain types of breaches occur (https://www.privacyrights.org/printpdf/67535). The actions are dependent on the type of data breached. In addition, as consumers, we should all continue to take proactive steps to protect ourselves online; see Appendix for *10 Steps to Protect Yourself Online*.

Defending Nation-State Cyberattacks

How should we defend ourselves from nation-state cyberattacks?

Nation state attacks are increasingly being directed at businesses and industrial facilities. Hackers are using sophisticated techniques to disrupt business operations and gather sensitive information. The threat increases as more and more digital devices are interconnected.

Ransomware and malware attacks such as WannaCry and NotPetya have spread globally, disrupting global shipping and production lines of U.S. companies. The availability of criminal and commercial malware is creating opportunities for new actors to launch cyber-operations against U.S. corporations.

---

[95] Jocelyn Baird, September 18th, 2018, A Year Later: What the 2017 Equifax Breach Taught Us, NextAdvisor, https://www.nextadvisor.com/blog/what-the-2017-equifax-breach-taught-us/

Chapter Eight: A New Path Forward

"Make no mistake, American companies are squarely in the cross-hairs of well-financed nation-state actors, who are routinely breaching private sector networks, stealing proprietary data, and compromising supply chains. The attacks are persistent, aggressive, and cost our nation jobs, economic advantage, and hundreds of billions of dollars."[96]

How does a corporation with a finite security budget and capability defend against these nation-state attacks? Here are a few suggestions:

1. Identify what information, capabilities or facilities would be of most use to a nation-state attacker. This will help focus where you need to be most vigilant in your security protective and detective measures

2. Ensure you are doing the basics right: keeping systems up-to-date and patched; using strong credential management; and securely configuring your network. These are the areas most nation-state attackers attempt to exploit first.

3. Constantly monitor security processes and network activity for suspicious behavior.

4. Reduce attack surfaces by limiting what is exposed to the Internet.

---

[96] Office of the Director of National Intelligence, January 7th, 2019, National Counterintelligence and Security Center Launches Campaign to Help Private Industry Guard Against Threats from Nation State Actors, https://www.dni.gov/index.php/ncsc-newsroom/item/1938-national-counterintelligence-and-security-center-launches-campaign-to-help-private-industry-guard-against-threats-from-nation-state-actors

5. Use encryption and media protection controls.

6. Educate users about phishing and ransomware. Perform periodic testing to evaluate user understanding and capabilities to spot suspicious emails and websites.

7. Institute restrictions and controls over employees traveling to certain "high risk" countries.

8. Review technology acquired from companies based in other "high risk" nations.

The U.S. National Counterintelligence and Security Center (NCSC) recently released a set of educational tools (videos, brochures and other materials) to help private sector businesses better protect themselves from cyber-attacks by nation-state actors.[97]

Since the 2017 Equifax Data Breach, there have been suggestions in the security community that the source of the attack was a nation state.

"CNBC talked to eight experts, including data "hunters" who scour the dark web for stolen information, senior cybersecurity managers, top executives at financial institutions, senior intelligence officials who played a part in the investigation and consultants who helped support it....none of them knows where the data is now. It's never appeared on any hundreds of underground websites selling stolen information. Security experts haven't seen the data used in any of the ways they'd

---

[97] See: https://www.dni.gov/index.php/ncsc-how-we-work/ncsc-know-the-risk-raise-your-shield/ncsc-awareness-materials

expect in a theft like this—not for impersonating victims, not for accessing other websites, nothing."[98]

There are two theories that try to explain why the massive data haul has not been seen in the dark web or appears to have been used in other ways.

One view is that the attackers were cyber-criminals and the data is "too hot" to sell on the dark web yet. It would draw the immediate attention of law enforcement so the criminals are holding onto the data for now. The other theory is that the data is in the hands of intelligence officers working for a foreign nation-state. As a former intelligence officer stated to CNBC:

"First...the foreign government is probably combining this information with other stolen data, then analyzing it using artificial intelligence or machine learning to figure out who's likely to be—or to become—a spy for the U.S. government. He pointed to other data breaches that focused on information that could be useful for identifying spies, such as a 2015 breach of the Office of Personnel Management, which processes the lengthy security clearance applications for U.S. government officials.

"Second, credit reporting data provides compromising information that can be used to turn valuable people into agents of a foreign government, influencers or, for lower-level employees, data thieves or informants. In particular, the credit information can be used to identify people in key

---

[98] Kate Fazzini, February 13th, 2019, The great Equifax mystery: seventeen months later, the stolen data has never been found, and experts are starting to suspect a spy scheme, CNBC, https://www.cnbc.com/2019/02/13/equifax-mystery-where-is-the-data.html

positions who have significant financial problems and could be compromised by bribes or high-paying jobs, the former official said. Financial distress is one of the most common reasons people commit espionage.

"The Equifax data provides information that could identify people who aren't even in these positions of influence yet, and could be valuable for years to come."[99]

* * * *

Some of our best lessons in life come from our mistakes. The Equifax 2017 Data Breach and other large data breaches provides you with a lot to think about as you apply these lessons to your company, team or family. For me, it has marked a turning point. I am using the information that I learned to help other companies improve their cybersecurity readiness and resilience. I am focusing my efforts on the Boards of Directors and senior leaders in corporations. It is this group that must make the important risk decisions and shape how their companies strategically address cybersecurity.

In my final chapter, I share some of the ways I am working with Boards and C-Suite (including the CISO) to improve cybersecurity.

---

[99] Ibid

Chapter Nine –
Improving Cybersecurity

When the Congressional report was released and my name was published all over the media and Internet, I really thought that that was the end of my professional career. But I was encouraged by friends and colleagues to look at this in a more positive light. They told me that I really had a lot to offer to others having been through one of the largest data breaches in history.

I have been fortunate to have lived through the entire process from the time of discovery through to the public announcement and the aftermath. My experience and lessons learned are valuable and can be shared with others. Leveraging this knowledge helps organizations better protect their assets and be better prepared to respond not if, but when, their companies are breached.

There is a lot of great work going on within companies by security and IT workers managing the day-to-day challenges of protecting and defending their systems from attack. But cybersecurity is still a relatively new field and not every CISO knows how to best communicate with senior management and the Board.

Conversely, many Board members and senior managers don't know what questions to ask or how to evaluate the answers they receive from their in-house cybersecurity experts. When I work with companies to help them improve their cybersecurity programs, I see four broad gaps that need to be addressed.

Educating Executives and Boards on Cybersecurity Risks and Trends

First and foremost, Boards and senior managers need to be able to understand the threats and emerging issues in cybersecurity to such a level that they feel comfortable asking questions and evaluating answers. The National Association of Corporate Directors Cybersecurity Oversight Principle 5 asks Boards to be able to discuss with management, including the identification of risks and how they are being treated and "specific plans associated with each approach."[100]

Much of the discussion that appears in the media and within the cybersecurity community is confusing. On one hand, an executive may read and hear about cyberwarfare and the fear, uncertainty and doubt about cybersecurity risks. On the other hand, they hear about mundane and technical issues that are difficult to understand or they cannot see how they apply to their company. What is lacking is robust discussion about actionable steps that Boards and senior managers should take to understand and address cyber-risks.

To be effective in discussions of cybersecurity risks, I believe that executives and Board members need to understand the following:

1. What are the most important information assets of the company?

---

[100] NACD Director's Handbook on Cyber-Risk Oversight (see page 163 footnote)

2. What are the cybersecurity and information security risks for each category of information assets and how is the company managing these?

3. What regulatory, compliance, and contractual requirements for cybersecurity and information security apply to the company?

4. How prepared is the company to respond to a cybersecurity or information security incident?

Let's look at each of these four areas in a little more detail.

What are the most important information assets of the company?[101]

Not all information in an organization has the same value. Trade Secrets, merger and acquisition discussions, pre-announcement financial data, new product development data, and consumer personal information would be considered highly sensitive. Compare this to marketing materials and information you disclose on your company website—often referred to as "public information."

Understanding the sensitivity or damage that would be caused if information were to be accessed by unauthorized persons or groups helps focus the cybersecurity discussion around how to protect that information.

---

[101] "Information" can also include non-digitized data and knowledge that may reside in the organization. While the focus here is on digitized data—data, files, documents that exist electronically in systems, databases, and data stores—management and Boards also need to consider the broader security of other non-digitized information.

The New Era of Cybersecurity Breaches

At a senior management level, I recommend that categories of information assets be identified and documented. Most companies maintain a classification scheme with three to five levels of sensitivity. Identifying all the information assets in an organization is not a simple task. It will often require security, information technology, legal, and business personnel working together to map out the business processes and data flows. A useful starting point is to list out all of the IT applications used by the company and the data held or processed in each application.

Next, you'll want to understand all the places where data is stored. These include network file shares, PC hard drives, internal websites ("intranet sites"), collaboration platforms, cloud file-sharing sites (such as Dropbox, Box, Google Drive, OneDrive).

There are automated tools to help discover files and documents in various data stores. There are also tools available to find copies of data that may reside outside of the systems designed to manage it. As data is identified, the inventory should also identify who has access to the data and the corresponding business justification. The inventory should also identify the owner of each application and data store.

The process of identifying data is an ongoing process in the organization, and someone in the organization should be responsible for maintaining the inventory. Also recognize that the data follows a life cycle. Some information might be highly sensitive to a point in time then become public data; a good example is a company's quarterly earnings statement. Up until its public release, only certain people need access to this information to prevent leak or inappropriate use of the data (such as using the data to trade in shares—i.e. insider trading). Once the information is made public, its sensitivity classification changes.

What are the cybersecurity and information security risks for each category of information assets and how is the company managing these risks?

Armed with an understanding of the types of data, its sensitivity, where it is located, and who has access to it and why, the Board and senior management should now seek to understand the key cybersecurity and information security risks. Risk is the potential of loss resulting from a given action. It is a function of threats, vulnerabilities, and the likelihood of threats acting against you. One of the primary roles of a Board and senior management team is to manage risk to protect the business and create an environment for it to grow and prosper.

There are many ways for an organization to identify its cybersecurity risks including:

1. External risk assessment study by a trusted cybersecurity consultant.
2. Use of risk assessment questionnaires and checklists.
3. Gap analysis of existing cybersecurity controls against best practices.
4. Vulnerability tests such as external penetration test and network scans.
5. Leveraging data from security event management tools.
6. Studying past breaches and security incidents to determine the likelihood of similar attacks against your company.
7. Subscribing to threat intelligence data services.

Risks should be recorded in a "risk register" for ongoing tracking. Not all risks carry equal significance or impact so there needs to be a way to categorize them; quantitative risk analysis uses hard metrics, such as dollars and is therefore considered more objective.

Qualitative risk analysis uses simple approximate values and is likely to be more subjective. Some risk models use a hybrid approach, combining elements of both by using quantitative analysis for risks which may be easily expressed in hard numbers (such as money), and qualitative for the remainder.

In my experience, the majority of companies utilize a qualitative approach to ranking risks. In this approach, judgment is used to rate the likelihood of the risk occurring against the impact on the company if the risk occurs.[102]

For example, consider an online store and the risk of external attack[103] by online criminals. The impact of this might be high as it could result in exposing customer identities and credit card numbers, and loss of confidence in the use of the store by customers. It could also cause monetary loss for the company and potential legal or regulatory actions.

The likelihood of this happening might also be considered high based on the frequency of data breaches occurring—remember there were 6,500 reported data breaches in 2018. So, in this example, the risk of external attack on the online store would be HIGH.

---

[102] There are many qualitative risk frameworks such as NIST SP800-30, CRAMM, FMEA/FMECA, CObIT

[103] "External attack" is a general description used here for illustrative purposes. The actual risk analysis might be more specific and identify different types of attacks (for example, SQL Injection, credential stuffing, denial of service, etc.)

Example Risk Assessment Matrix Used for Qualitative Risk Assessment

	Impact		
Likelihood	**Low**	**Medium**	**High**
Low	Low	Low	Medium
Medium	Low	Medium	High
High	Medium	High	High

Qualitative risk assessment is generally faster and less expensive than quantitative methods but many question the ability of qualitative models to truly convey cybersecurity risks.

Some organizations prefer to use more precise quantitative methods to assess cybersecurity risk. These methods started being used in government computer systems but were not widely adopted in the private sector. Quantitative methods are receiving more focus as CISOs seek to find better ways to communicate risks to senior managers and Boards.

The most common quantitative method is to calculate the ALE (Annualized Loss Expectancy) of each asset and then sum all these values to arrive at an overall company-wide risk calculation. The ALE is calculated as follows: ALE = SLE x ARO. The SLE (Single Loss Expectancy) or expected loss of an incident is calculated using an estimate of the asset value (in dollars) and the risk exposure (expressed as a probability): SLE = asset value X the risk exposure. ARO (Annualized Rate of Occurrence) is an estimate of times per year that an incident might occur. Using the same example from above for the online store:

Asset value[104]: $100m
Risk exposure: 1 (or 100%)
Annualized rate of occurrence: 0.5

So the ALE would be $50m ($50m=[100m x 1] x 0.5). This means that in the event of a successful attack on the online store, you would expect to an annual loss of $50m. This could then be evaluated against the costs of deploying protective and defensive processes and tools to better secure the online store.

Another model receiving increasing focus is FAIR (Factor Analysis Information Risk). FAIR underlines that risk is an uncertain event and one should not focus on what is possible, but on how probable is a given event. This probabilistic approach is applied to every factor that is analyzed.

In *How to Measure Anything in Cybersecurity Risk,* authors Douglas Hubbard and Richard Seiesen advocate strongly for a more qualitative approach to measuring cybersecurity risk; they "offer an alternative to a set of deeply rooted risk assessment methods now widely used in cybersecurity but that have no basis in the mathematics of risk or scientific method…. These methods impede decisions about a subject

---

[104] There are several steps in determining an asset value.

of growing criticality."[105] They argue that quantitative methods used to measure risk in other fields can be applied to cybersecurity:

"We also argue that methods based on real evidence of improving decisions are not only practical but already have been applied to a wide variety of equally difficult problems...avoiding problems inherent to "risk matrices" and "risk scores."[106]

Regardless of how risk is identified and presented to the Board and senior management, they must be able to understand how the company is dealing with key cybersecurity risks. There are four commonly-used approaches when dealing with risk: mitigate, transfer, accept or avoid.[107]

---

[105] Douglas W. Hubbard & Richard Seiersen, 2016, How to Measure Anything in Cybersecurity Risk, John Wiley & Sons, Inc. (ISBN: 978-1-119-08529-4)

[106] Ibid

[107] Not discussed here is how companies can quantitatively measure the risk treatment approaches applied to risks, to arrive at a net risk score.

Cybersecurity Risk Treatments

Mitigate	Transfer	Accept	Avoid
Implement a measure to reduce or virtually eliminate the risk	Share the cost of something going wrong with another party	Ignore the risk or decide not to take any action to address the risk	Remove the underlying cause of the risk
Most frequently used in cybersecurity.	*Note that you never really transfer the risk, just the impact*	*May be used when cost to address outweighs the impact of the risk occurring*	*Often used to eliminate cybersecurity risks*
Examples: Fix a vulnerability by applying a patch or upgrading a system Implement a compensating (e.g. encrypting data in a database)	Example: Cyber insurance coverage for a data breach	Example: Approved policy exception	Examples: Shut down or upgrade a system Delete data Cease (or decide not to do) business with a third party

In most cases, companies will choose to mitigate key risks by applying various technical, procedural and human controls to reduce the risk to an acceptable level. A company may decide to accept risks at a certain risk level (e.g., low or medium) especially when the cost to apply mitigating controls outweighs the potential impact.[108] When a decision is made to accept a risk, this should be documented in the company's risk register and approved by senior management, with full knowledge of the risk being accepted.

Understanding risks and treatments will also help the Board in evaluating the various disclosures required by the Securities & Exchange Commission related to cybersecurity risk.[109]

What regulatory, compliance, and contractual requirements for cybersecurity and information security apply to the company?

I am a big fan of taking a risk-based approach to cybersecurity, but there is always a compliance aspect that must be considered. Compliance refers to specific requirements that must be met by the company, these requirements coming from federal or state legislation, regulatory bodies, industry organizations, or major customers. The cybersecurity program needs to ensure it meets these requirements. Failure to meet requirements can result in regulatory actions, fines, and class action lawsuits. It is important that the senior management and Board understand the general requirements the company has under these various compliance mandates, and how they are being addressed by the company.

---

[108] The same may apply when the time to mitigate is lengthy. Managers may decide to "wait it out" until a better solution becomes available, thus deciding to accept the risk for a period of time.

[109] See Chapter 8.

Here is a list of some of the typical legal and regulatory requirements your company may need to comply with:

1. Sarbanes-Oxley Act 2002 deals with controls over financial reporting. Requires quarterly and annual certifications on internal controls, including IT controls. Does not include specific cybersecurity requirements but internal controls include how changes are made to, and access is managed for, financial reporting systems.

2. Health Insurance Portability and Accountability Act 1996 (HIPAA) deals with the privacy and security of personally identifiable health information managed by health providers and insurance companies.

3. Financial Modernization Act 1999 (frequently referred to as the Gram-Leach-Bliley Act or GLBA) has requirements for privacy and security related to providers of financial services products, generally banks and financial institutions.

4. Payment Card Industry Data Security Standards (PCI-DSS) are industry security standards for merchants who process credit card transactions. When a merchant processes a certain volume of transactions, it must obtain a PCI audit and certification.

5. State privacy legislation that places requirements on protection of consumer personal information and notification in the event of a data breach.

6. International laws and regulations including the European General Data Privacy Regulation (GDPR).

How prepared is the company to respond to a cybersecurity or information security incident?

The Board of Directors and senior management need to be able to evaluate how well a company will respond in a time of crisis when controls have failed and a potential or actual cyber-incident is identified.

Some of the key questions and discussions for the Board include:

1. Is there a documented incident response playbook?

2. Do the Board and senior management understand their respective roles in a major incident?

3. Have communication protocols, including templated press releases, employee communications, and consumer notices been prepared?

4. Who, and how, will law enforcement and government agencies be notified?

5. How are we training and exercising our team members in the cybersecurity incident response plans?

6. Have we identified what constitutes a material cyber-security event?

I encourage cybersecurity leaders to provide ongoing training and awareness sessions for their Board and senior management. I have supported these efforts by leading on-site and virtual training courses on various cybersecurity topics. These are designed for business leaders without a lot of technical jargon. They focus on equipping Board members and senior managers with the tools and knowledge they need to fulfill their responsibilities as stewards of the company's resources.

Improving Cybersecurity Strategies

According to a survey by PWC in 2018, "forty-four percent of the 9,500 executives in 122 countries surveyed...say they do not have an overall information security strategy."[110]

Every company needs a cybersecurity strategy. Why? Because you cannot defend against every cybersecurity threat that exists. You need to make choices. You need to identify your risks and manage them, consistent with your corporate strategy and risk appetite. Strategy is about making choices. Your cybersecurity strategy is an integral part of your overall business strategy and should identify what you want to do and how you will get there.

I have reviewed and developed many cybersecurity strategy documents over my career. The best ones are simple documents that clearly define the overall direction, prioritize key initiatives, and include a broad roadmap over a three-[111] to five-year timeline. To develop a cybersecurity strategy, I recommend:

Understand the current state - a good place to start is to take a look in the mirror and do an honest assessment of where the business is right

---

[110] PWC Study (see page 63 footnote)

[111] I encourage clients to use a three-year plan horizon. Five years tends to be too far out to make meaningful estimates and projections of what might change in the business and cybersecurity environment.

now and your current cybersecurity profile. A couple of useful tools can be used here. One is a SWOT analysis where you look at your business and cybersecurity strengths, weaknesses, opportunities and threats.

Another option is to assess your cybersecurity posture against a security framework such as ISO 27002, CObIT, CIS Top 20, or the NIST Cybersecurity Framework. If you have additional regulatory or legal mandates, it might also be useful to look at those compliance frameworks to identify any significant gaps.

Using one or more of these tools will help you assess your company against industry best practice. You don't want to spend too much time looking at your current state; it is easy to spend a lot of time here.

Understand the resources available - what information, plans, technology, personnel, financial and third-party resources do you have available to work with as you build your future plans? Knowing what you have (or can obtain) will determine how feasible it is to implement your strategy.

Understand the Company's future state vision - now you need to understand (or help define) the overall company vision. Most companies state their vision, mission and core values in simple, easily understood sentences or documents. Where does cybersecurity fit within the overall vision, mission and values of the organization? Understanding this linkage will be important in determining goals, objectives and roadmap.

Define Goals, Objectives and Roadmap - the final step in developing the cybersecurity strategy is to define your goals (what you want to accomplish) and your objectives (specific, measurable, attainable actions that you will achieve and when). Goals and objectives should be developed that directly support the company vision, mission and core values. They must also be realistic based on the resources available or that you can obtain.

After defining goals and objectives, you can then lay out your objectives (or groups of objectives) on a high-level timeline or roadmap. This is not intended to be a project plan but rather a high-level timeline that can be used to communicate the sequence of activities that will be needed over, say, a three-year time horizon. Your cybersecurity strategy becomes a living document and should be updated at least once per year. Many of my client CISOs conduct an annual review of their strategy with the senior management team and Board of Directors.

Developing strategy documents is not necessarily a core competency of a cybersecurity leader. Engaging a cybersecurity consultant to assist you in developing or updating your cybersecurity strategy may be worthwhile. An independent consultant can help bring ideas from other clients, help craft the key themes and messages, and provide guidance on how to sell the strategy to senior management. Boards and senior managers might use an independent consultant to validate and provide feedback on the cybersecurity strategy developed by their team. I really enjoy it when I see a security team develop a great cybersecurity plan and successfully pitch it to their senior management and Board. It really focuses the discussion around the risks and allows the Board to make the important risk decisions that will guide the future investments in cybersecurity.

Improving Cybersecurity Response and Resilience

According to a recent PWC study, forty-eight percent of 9,500 executives in 122 countries surveyed, say they do not have an employee awareness training program, and 54% say they do not have an incident response process.[112]

Few Board members feel very confident that their companies are properly secured against cyberattacks. The National Association of Corporate Directors reports that only 5% of public-company and 4% of private-company directors said they were "very confident" their companies were properly secured against cyberattacks. Most (42% of public companies and 39% of private companies) felt "moderately confident."[113]

I believe Boards and senior management need to approach the cybersecurity space with the expectation that they have been or will be attacked. This should drive them to start asking questions of their team in three areas:

1. What are the company's capabilities to prevent and detect threat actors and possible security incidents?

2. How is the company able to react and respond in the event of a cybersecurity incident?

3. How resilient are our business operations, processes and technology in the event of a major cybersecurity event?

---

[112] PWC Study (see page 63 footnote)
[113] NACD Director's Handbook on Cyber-Risk Oversight (see page 163 footnote)

Prevention and Detection

Company management should implement a combination of procedural, human and technological controls to properly secure the key assets of the organization. The specific controls implemented should align with the organization's assessment of risk.

Specific areas that should be covered, include:

1. Limiting access to physical and logical assets and associated facilities to authorized users, processes, and devices.

2. Training and educating employees, contractors, and business partners on their cybersecurity-related duties and responsibilities.

3. Implementing technical controls to protect the confidentiality, integrity, and availability of information and records (data).

4. Publishing and maintaining security policies and procedures and implementing processes to ensure compliance with the policies and procedures.

5. Managing and monitoring technical security solutions on an ongoing basis to ensure the security and resilience of systems and assets, and detection of anomalous activity.

6. Maintaining continuous monitoring and detection processes and procedures to verify the effectiveness of protective measures and ensure awareness of anomalous events.

Response

With appropriate prevention and detection strategies and controls in place, your company should be well-equipped to identify when a potential cybersecurity incident occurs. Now you need to have a well-documented and practiced response process to enable your organization to quickly determine the impact and resolution of the incident.

I encourage every organization to have a written response plan. Writing down the process and procedures helps clarify roles and responsibilities and builds a common understanding of what activities need to occur in the event of a cybersecurity incident. The written plan can then be tested and practiced using various scenarios and simulations.

The typical sequence of activities is as follows:

1. Security event is identified.
2. Event is analyzed and investigated to determine if it is a "false positive" or actual cybersecurity incident.
3. Incident is declared and response process is activated.
4. Response activities activated (many performed concurrently), including:
    a. Blocking or mitigating the threat,
    b. Identifying impact,
    c. Understanding cause,
    d. Performing remediation,
    e. Implementing enhanced controls,
    f. Notifications.
5. Incident is debriefed and response plans updated as necessary.

An important part of the organization's response capability is ensuring the appropriate communications occur. There should be a clear understanding about the roles and responsibilities of various stakeholders, including senior management and the Board.

Resilience

Resilience is the ability of the IT systems and business processes to withstand a major disruption within acceptable degradation parameters and to recover within an acceptable time. Basically, it acknowledges that cybersecurity (or other disruptive) events occur regularly and systems and processes should be designed in such a way as to minimize the impact, maybe with some short-term degradation. Systems and business processes should be able to "bounce back" quickly from any cybersecurity incident and be stronger as a result of the incident.

Company management should be ensuring they design their IT systems and business processes in such a way that they are resilient. This concept of resilience has become more prominent in the last few years as the modern enterprise has become more and more dependent on technology. When I started consulting, I helped companies develop "disaster recovery plans." These later became referred to as "business continuity plans."

I still relish the challenge of helping firms in this way today, and no two consultancy tasks are the same, so I see it as my responsibility to ensure every client company is kept up and running.

Indeed, inherent in these earlier approaches was an acceptance that the company operations could be down for some period of time—referred to as the "recovery time objective or RTO." For many businesses today, even being down for a few minutes is unacceptable.

We do not need to accept that a business will be "down" for any extended period, and this is where hiring a coach or consultant is a critical action—and to do this proactively (before a disaster can occur), not reactively, when it happens.

Cyber resilience is as much a way of thinking as it is a set of specific practices or actions that can be taken. Taking a cyber-resilient approach helps businesses to recognize that bad actors have the advantage of innovative tools, the element of surprise, the ability to target specific points of failure, and can be successful in their attempts. With this recognition, you can implement appropriate controls to prevent, detect, respond and rapidly recover to the intended secure state. It requires management to think differently about cybersecurity and be more agile in handling cybersecurity incidents.

I encourage Boards and senior managers to engage in a dialog about how cyber-resilient the organization is today and what can be done to improve the organization's resilience. Implementing appropriate controls for protection, detection and response is certainly an important part. Other specific approaches I have seen include:

1. Using secure system design principles in building new systems that anticipate attacks and minimize their impact.
2. Enhancing the automation of vulnerability identification and remediation (orchestration).
3. Implementing critical data recovery capabilities.
4. Reducing legacy systems' risks.
5. Increasing the use of the public cloud to run systems.

6. Building resilience into business operations and processes.
7. Learning from other case studies where companies suffered a significant loss of operations.

The World Economic Forum released a paper in 2017, *Advancing Cyber Resilience Principles and Tools for Boards*[114] that provides ten principles that should be applied to help develop a cyber-resilient organization. The framework is a useful resource for Boards to review when engaging in a discussion on cyber resilience.

Mentoring and Coaching Board Members, Senior Leaders and CISOs

The National Association of Corporate Directors Report on Cybersecurity Oversight concluded:

"As the cyber threat has grown, the responsibility (and expectations) of Board members has grown also. Directors need to do more than simply understand that threats exist and receive reports from management. They need to employ the same principles of inquiry and constructive-challenge that are standard features of Board management discussions about strategy and company performance."[115]

---

[114] World Economic Forum, January 2017, Advancing Cyber Resilience Principles and Tools for Boards, http://www3.weforum.org/docs/IP/2017/Adv_Cyber_Resilience_Principles-Tools.pdf

[115] NACD Director's Handbook on Cyber-Risk Oversight (see page 163 footnote)

Let's face it, we can all improve our knowledge, skills and capabilities. If you are a Board member and feel you could learn more about cybersecurity so you can engage in the kind of detailed "inquiry and constructive-challenge" expected of you within this role, why not get a personal coach to help you learn, find resources, and be better equipped to fulfil your obligations? A coach is your independent, trusted advisor who can work with you to help develop the cybersecurity knowledge you need.

There has been much discussion about requiring a cyber expert on each Board of Directors. There has even been legislation introduced to require cybersecurity expertise in the boardroom, similar to the requirement to have financial accounting experience on the Board. The NACD report concluded: "Proposals aimed, for example, at requiring all Boards to have a director who is a "cybersecurity expert"—even setting aside the fact that the severe shortage of senior-level cybersecurity talent, with hundreds of thousands of positions vacant in the U.S. alone, makes such proposals impossible to implement..."[116] A coach gives you on-demand access to the type of cybersecurity expertise you need when required.

The Council of Institutional Investors published in 2016 five questions that investors should ask directors about cybersecurity. One question stated: "How does the Board evaluate the effectiveness of the company's cybersecurity efforts?"[117] Inherent in this question is that the Board has the knowledge and capabilities to be able to evaluate the

---

[116] Ibid

[117] Council for Institutional Investors, April 2016, Prioritizing Cybersecurity: Five Investor Questions for Portfolio Company Boards, https://www.cii.org/files/publications/misc/4-27-16%20Prioritizing%20Cybersecurity.pdf

strategy. Using an outside cybersecurity advisor is a useful way to help the Board in its evaluation activities.

There is a worldwide shortage of security professionals. According to (ISC)², a non-profit that focuses on cybersecurity certifications, there were over 2.9 million open security positions worldwide in 2018, with 500,000 open jobs in North America[118]. I expect these shortages and gaps in cybersecurity to continue for several years.

Even more challenging is finding a CISO ready to have a seat at the CEO table. If you are a large organization, you may have the resources to attract the right person. However, most companies still struggle with finding a CISO able to lead a security team and operate as part of a senior management team. Often, this leads to frustration either on the part of the senior managers, the CISO or both, contributing to generally high turnover in many CISO positions. The average tenure of CISOs is eighteen months. Some smaller organizations do not even have a CISO or are unable to attract the right type of person for that role.

Given these challenges, I am often asked to work with CISOs to help them be more effective leaders and managers. While each engagement is unique, there are some common areas where coaching has been most useful to CISOs and senior security executives, including:

1. Understanding organizational dynamics and developing influencing skills.
2. Positioning the optimal reporting models and structure.

---

[118] ISC2, 2018, Cybersecurity Professionals Focus on Developing New Skills as Workforce Gap Widens: (ISC)² Cybersecurity Workforce Study, 2018, https://www.isc2.org/-/media/ISC2/Research/2018-ISC2-Cybersecurity-Workforce-Study.ashx?la=en&hash=4E09681D0FB51698D9BA6BF13EEABFA48BD17DB0

3. Building effective metrics and measures for senior managers and Boards.
4. Honing executive presentations and conducting courageous discussions.
5. Making the transition from technical manager to influencer.
6. Measuring and educating senior leaders on the business value of security.
7. Using cybersecurity as a value-adder rather than a value-detractor.

For me, there is nothing more encouraging than to see a company where the CISO is a respected member of the senior leadership, working alongside business and technology leaders, and enabling the business to move forward with the right cybersecurity controls. In these forward-thinking organizations, cybersecurity is just an integral part of doing business.

Cybersecurity enables the business to grow by working hand-in-hand with the business leaders, allowing those leaders to take informed risks. Managers and employees understand their respective roles in protecting the company's data assets and defending them from attack. When something goes wrong, the company has the response plans and processes to react quickly, minimizing the impacts, and quickly returning to a steady-state.

* * * *

Wherever you are on your cybersecurity journey, I trust that you have learned something from this book and the 2017 Equifax Data Breach. At the very least, you may have identified some areas where your cybersecurity program could be improved.

The threats and technologies are always changing; I encourage you to constantly review and evaluate your cybersecurity program. Ensure you focus on people, process and technology equally—all must work together to effectively protect, detect and respond to cybersecurity threats.

Good luck!

Appendix—10 Tips to Protect Your Personal Information

10 TIPS TO PROTECT YOUR PERSONAL INFORMATION

Use strong and unique passwords for online accounts. Make your password complex and unpredictable by using a mix of letters, numbers, and symbols. Better yet, use a password manager to generate and securely store your passwords.

 **Close unused accounts.** Some of these accounts may contain personal information that would be valuable to an identity thief. Eliminate the risk by closing old email accounts, online shopping and service provider accounts you no longer use. The less personal information stored online about you, the better.

Be cautious of public Wi-Fi. Most free public Wi-Fi networks offer little or no security. Someone could monitor or eavesdrop on what you are doing online. Don't access sensitive sites like your bank when on a public Wi-Fi network. Consider using a VPN (virtual private network) if you must use public networks.

Limit social media sharing. The more personal information you post, the more information you provide to an identity thief to enable the thief to impersonate you. Limit sharing to a small group of people. Check your social media privacy settings.

Freeze your credit report. Placing a "security freeze" on your credit report prevents others accessing it, for example to run a credit check to open a new account. This is now free and relatively simple with Equifax, Experian and TransUnion. You will need to unfreeze your credit report to allow others to verify your credit.

Avoid opening emails from untrusted sources or unusual attachments. This is a common method used by hackers to gain access to your systems or data. Don't click on attachments or links that look suspicious, even if it appears to come from someone you know. If something seems off, don't click it.

Back-up your data. If your computer is taken over by ransomware, you may lose all your data. There are many online services that provide regular backups of your computer data and documents. For extra important data, consider a periodic hardware backup also.

 **Keep software updated**. Vendors provide frequent system updates for your computer, phone and other devices. Install these updates quickly as they may close a security vulnerability that could allow an attacker to access your device or data.

Keep your offline information secure. Store your personal documents in a safe place in your home. Do not leave wallets or personal documents in public view. Shred personal documents when they are no longer needed. Destroy labels on prescription bottles before you dispose of them.

 **Review your credit report.** You are entitled to a free credit report each year from each of the three national credit reporting agencies (Equifax, Experian, and TransUnion). Review each report in detail to see if there are any unusual accounts listed. If there are, you may be a victim of identity theft - follow the steps at identitytheft.gov.

C4E CYBERSECURITY for EXECUTIVES

Please contact me if I can be of help in any way. There is nothing more fulfilling than assisting a client to prevent their own data breach disaster, and I will always advise where I can.

 cybersecurity4executives.com

 @Cybersecurity4E

 linkedin.com/in/payneg

 graeme@cybersecurity4executives.com

 +1 (404)-429-7512

About the Author

Graeme Payne is a consultant, speaker and coach. He works with boards and senior executives to help them understand and manage cybersecurity and IT risks. He has over 30 years' experience in consulting and IT management in financial services, insurance, healthcare, retail, manufacturing and utility industries. During the Equifax 2017 Data Breach (which exposed the sensitive information on 146 million US consumers), he was Senior Vice President and CIO of Global Corporate Platforms. He was fired the day before the former Chairman and CEO of Equifax testified to Congress that the root cause of the data breach was a human error and technological failure. Graeme would later be identified as "the human error".

Prior to joining Equifax in 2011, Graeme was a Principal at Ernst & Young and Global Leader of Governance, Risk & Compliance at Wipro Consulting. Over his 30-year career he has consulted with hundreds of companies on cybersecurity and IT risk programs. Graeme started his career as an accountant and holds several security and IT risk certifications. He grew up and worked in New Zealand before moving to the United States in 1995.

Made in the USA
Columbia, SC
25 September 2022

67659737R00136